SOLVING

THE SALES MANAGER/

SALES AUTOMATION

EQUATION

BY TIMOTHY MCMAHON

DARTNELL is a publisher serving the world of business with book manuals, newsletters and bulletins, and training materials for executives, managers, supervisors, salespeople, financial officials, personnel executives, and office employees. Dartnell also produces management and sales training videos and audiocassettes, publishes many useful business forms, and many of its materials and films are available in languages other than English. Dartnell, established in 1917, serves the world's business community. For details, catalogs, and product information, write:

THE DARTNELL CORPORATION
4660 N. Ravenswood Ave.
Chicago, IL 60640-4595, U.S.A.
or phone (800) 621-5463 in U.S. and Canada

Copyright 1996 in the United States, Canada, and Britain by
THE DARTNELL CORPORATION
Library of Congress Catalog Card Number: 96-083842
ISBN 0-85013-252-5

Printed in the United States of America

DEDICATION

To Casey, Katie, Tim, & Betsy
… the best of the best

Fill your lives with the Burning Desire
to Know, to Connect, to Transcend

ACKNOWLEDGMENTS

I want to give special thanks to my wife, Susan, whose amazing faith in even the most difficult times gave me the courage to go out on my own and to write this book. She deserves the credit.

Thanks to Chris Heide at Dartnell, a good friend who had much to do with making this project possible. Also many thanks to Kerri Wallace-Reilly, a long-time friend who also believes and to Lorraine DePolo for her insight and critical eye.

I also want to express my appreciation to Howard Getson and Doug Fenn at IntellAgent Control for their invaluable contribution, and to Andre Crump and Carol Francavilla at Apple Computer.

Finally, thanks to my good friends, "The Elegants" — you know who you are.

TABLE OF CONTENTS

SOLVING THE SALES MANAGER/SALES AUTOMATION EQUATION TOOLKIT IN MICROSOFT WORD 2.0

Instructions:

Start your word processor.
Insert the diskette in your floppy drive.
Click on file, Open.
Change to the a:\drive.
Change directories to the toolkit directory.
Select the file you want to open.
Click on OK.

This diskette does not contain software. This diskette contains documents you can use with a word processor that reads Microsoft Word 2.0 formatted documents.

Toolkit Topics:

1.	Financial Justification	finjust.doc
2.	Field and Sales Effectiveness Survey	effsurv.doc
3.	SFA Strategic Plan	sfaplan.doc
4.	Sales Needs Questionnaire	prequest.doc
5.	STRATEGY MAPPING Forms	smforms.doc

FOREWORD

SELLING 2000 — The Vision and the Promise of Sales Automation first appeared in paperback early in 1994. Since then many of its concepts and ideas have become a part of mainstream thinking about sales automation, and it has been called "required reading for every CEO in America." The critical success factors for sales automation which it identified, specifically the importance and critical role of sales management in sales automation, are today better understood, as are the potential benefits to the *company as a whole*, not just the salesperson.

Still, the sales automation industry is a young one. There is much experimentation, and some sales organizations are on their second or even third reimplementation — applying what they have learned, often by trial and error, to build *systems* that will play an increasingly more effective role in leveraging corporate success.

When I wrote *Selling 2000*, I honestly felt at the time that it said most of what could be said about sales automation. But for every one question that it answered, two or three new ones have arrived to take its place, each seeking a whole new set of answers. If there is one concept of sales automation that we are just now really understanding is how interrelated automation technology and selling methodology are and how creating logical links between the two opens whole new vistas of the potential of sales automation. Along with this, we continue to recognize just how critical sales managers are. They are becoming even more necessary to manage corporate change and we are recognizing the need to better define the benefits to them and equip them with the tools they need to manage business in today's new selling environment.

So two years later, and as part of a much broader work, *Solving the Sales Manager/Sales Automation Equation*, I find myself building upon *Selling 2000* throughout this book — expanding on some "old" ideas that are still absolute truths and adding many new ideas that show just how much we've learned and perhaps point the way to the future. I continue to be challenged by this thing we call "sales force automation" that, like this book, is really a continuing work-in-progress. To paraphrase the philosophers, as great as the goals are, it is perhaps that journey itself that is the most exciting.

CHAPTER 1

SELLING 2000 — A SALES AUTOMATION PRIMER

By now, most everyone who is directly or even indirectly in sales has heard about sales force automation (SFA). Just a few short years ago, attendees at sales conferences and trade shows would approach vendor booths and ask, "So what is this sales automation thing?" Today, however, SFA is a major topic of sales industry conferences and "how-to" seminars, and it is regularly covered in the press. SFA vendors continue to refine their software systems and add new capabilities—some of which challenge our ability to make use of them all!

Salespeople, managers, and company executives are beginning to really understand the inevitable changes technology will bring to the business of selling and servicing customers. Perhaps most important is the understanding that realizing the fullest potential of sales force automation will require much more than simply providing salespeople with notebook computers and sophisticated software. Success will encompass new processes, methodologies, and even behavioral issues, as well as coping with and accepting much change.

But there is a paradox in sales automation. In a national poll, the *number one* information systems project of the Fortune 1000 was sales automation, defined as the creation and implementation of sophisticated communications networks with sales productivity software, remote computer systems, and other tools. (Today more than 1000 vendors—an ever-increasing number—compete in this emerging marketplace.)

By contrast, this interest *continues* to build despite a 1993 study that described 85% of all SFA implementations since 1983 (when the industry effectively began) as less than fully successful. In other words, **buyers did not fully realize the results they expected going in.** As one corporate executive put it:

> We understand now our mistake. We began with **technology**, equipping the sales force with computers and SFA software. We followed that with **information**, filling the databases with all the data we thought a salesperson would ever need or want to track. We forgot about **process**, that is, defining exactly what we wanted them to do with all that computing power and data. We somehow thought the reps would figure that out for themselves. Apparently they didn't ... or wouldn't!
>
> This time around we're reversing the sequence. **Process** is first to understand and define what we want our salespeople to do differently for greater success ... and how. Then we're going to select just the **information** really needed to support that process. Finally we're going to look at automation **technology** as a means to deliver that information and support the process. That will work!

PROCESS BEFORE TECHNOLOGY

How important is process before technology to the sales automation equation? It is unique to automation that just using the hardware and software consistently will not necessarily produce quality results. Automating sales is unlike automating the traditional business applications such as accounting, manufacturing, distribution, and so forth — applications in which computerization directly brings routine, substantial increases in productivity and efficiency. Traditional business applications respond very well to computerization because they are already based on firmly defined and consistently applied *processes*, such as standard accounting practices or manufacturing methods.

THE COMPUTERIZATION PRINCIPLE:
It is the inherent nature of computer systems that they effectively automate processes; they are only a reflection of the process, however, not the creator!

Given this principle, it makes sense that a sales automation system can only be as effective as the underlying sales and management processes that it reflects or supports. And if there are no *formal* or consistent processes in place or, not uncommonly, no known processes at all, the results (or lack of results) are predictable.

As in the "traditional" business applications, automation plays an interesting role in *validating* processes. Because of its computerized ability to speed up the process and because it delivers increasingly accurate and real-time data, valid processes visibly work better and faulty processes work worse. As such, when SFA doesn't produce the expected results — or even causes negative results — that can challenge many long-held and previously unassailable corporate assumptions and beliefs (sometimes generating the defensive response, "It couldn't be the process; there must be something wrong with the software"). Hmm. ...

It's not that sales does not have processes. It usually has too complicated a process or too many different processes that are inconsistent across the organization. Processes are too complex, burdensome, or paper intensive; or everyone is "doing their own thing"; or several different sales methodologies are in use simultaneously across the organization.

For sales automation to work, just like any other business application, there has to be agreement on a single, universal process.

Imagine, for example, a company that used different accounting methods in each of its locations while attempting to do integrated financial planning. Chaos! And that's exactly what happens with SFA.

The "process dilemma" extends far beyond sales. We know that SFA's broader potential is the linking of sales with the other areas of the business that need sales information and vice versa. These include marketing, customer service, pre- and post-sale support, and other company functions. Doing so effectively will again, however, require common or at least complementary processes that can allow each of these business functions to work together more effectively.

But instead of each of these organizations sharing information, working together, using common processes, and being linked by technology, today we have plenty of good people, all doing their jobs in their own way (or as specified by their management). Rather than working with "hard facts" upon which to make better and more coordinated customer decisions, they do the best they can too often with spotty information. And sometimes things do just fall through the cracks. The growing trend toward the virtual office (closing offices and having people work from home) is making this kind of necessary cross-functional communication even more difficult and more critical.

So sales automation's successes or shortcomings have not been, in large part, due so much to the inadequacies of technology as to the inadequacies of planning, the lack of direction, and the realistic understanding of the true success factors, especially the role of process. Not unusual in an emerging industry.

Today the technology is more readily available, affordable, and more proven — a far cry from just a few years ago. The real challenge ahead will be in how sales automation is *applied* to sales and corporate organizations and the fundamental structural and cultural changes in the fabric of the corporation it will make.

MYTHS AND REALITIES

A good place to start is to look at some of the *myths* of selling and sales automation and some of the new *realities*.

MYTH: We must automate!
REALITY: We must solve business issues!

The myth is that to stay competitive in today's market we *must* automate our salespeople. At a recent conference I heard a speaker say that we must all "get with the new technologies of selling or be left behind."

I don't disagree with that statement, but we should pose the following questions, "What happens if we make a major investment in hardware and software and the reps don't (or won't) use it? What if they just don't feel that it's providing much of a return-on-investment to them? What *exactly* is it that we want the reps to do with it?"

The reality is that we must figure out exactly what set of *business problems* we want to solve with sales automation. We must define exactly which set of actions will produce the desired results and how technology can best support the execution of those actions.

We do know now that certain business issues are responding well to sales automation technology. The following are a few examples:

1. Lead Management and Focus Marketing.

The combination of telequalifying and automated rapid fulfillment, followed by electronic lead distribution of "prequalified" leads to the sales force has proven its value. The competitive benefits of quick lead follow-up and focusing the salespeople only on leads with a higher potential are clear. More advanced systems integrating data analysis reporting, mapping, and similar tools in the hands of business-savvy salespeople are even further enhancing sales productivity and effectiveness. Tracking of lead progress and success by analytical marketing professionals is allowing them to fine-tune marketing programs based on real-world response patterns. One way to view this is to think of "reshaping" the sales funnel or pipeline.

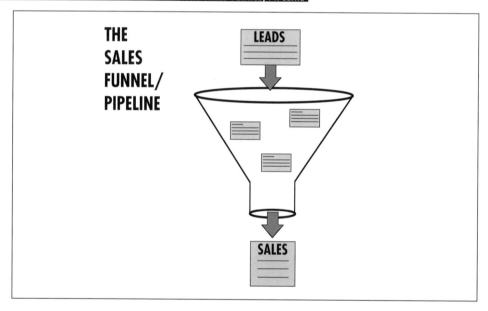

FIGURE 1.1. LEAD MANAGEMENT: RESHAPING THE SALES FUNNEL/PIPELINE

As shown in the illustrations, sales pipelines are often represented as a funnel in which new "suspects" are continuously added to the top. If you put in enough at the top, you'll get enough closed business coming out the bottom—or so the theory goes. In practice, however, adding more and more suspects to the funnel (that is, *expanding* the top) has the opposite effect of *narrowing* the bottom. In short, putting more in can actually *reduce* the amount of closed business produced!

FIGURE 1.2

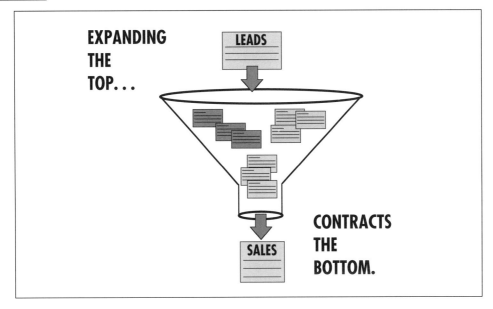

One reason this happens is because each lead or suspect entered into the system creates *overhead*; that is, each requires that a certain amount of time be spent to service and fulfill the lead, and to qualify or disqualify it. Additionally, too many leads, even if qualified, use up the salesperson's most valuable and limited resource—time—and can limit his or her ability to focus efforts on the highest potential sales opportunities. So we can end up with lots of execution of limited quality.

FIGURE 1.3

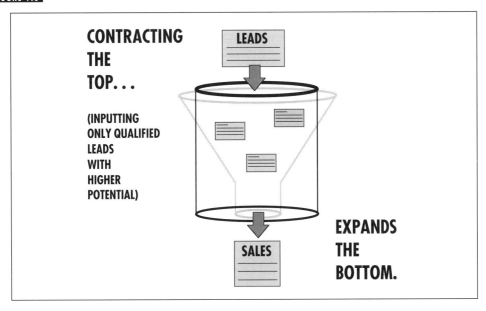

As this illustration shows, to maximize sales results and increase closed business, we need to *reshape* the funnel to a more pipelike shape—first by *contracting* the top by adding fewer, better potential opportunities. As we've said, many companies are accomplishing this with new *telequalifying* departments that utilize sales automation to screen and qualify leads with electronic lead distribution of "turnovers" (the highest quality leads). This results in the *expansion* of the bottom or increased sales. In other words, we make more of the salespeople's time available for the highest *quality of execution* on the highest *quality* of business.

2. Forecast Accuracy and Corporate Planning.

This *could* be the big payoff in the long term for sales automation. Consider the key decisions made at least indirectly on sales forecast data (which, as we all know, are notoriously inaccurate). Fundamentally, forecast data are used to decide to expand or contract businesses, to hire new people or lay them off, to offer new products and services or eliminate those that are not selling, and to manage manufacturing capability, finished goods, and raw materials inventories—all of which directly impact our ability to provide high levels of customer satisfaction. All these decisions are at least in part based on that same information.

Maintaining and improving the customer service level is always a key corporate goal with direct impact on sales. What is the potential benefit to *any* company of being able to plan the precise minimum amount of resources necessary to achieve the highest possible customer service level? It is possible. With SFA technology across the company, we can now know what is in the sales pipeline and how it will translate into needed resources. We are also able to track the progress (and process) of the sale, while continually assessing its viability and adjusting plans.

For example, imagine the potential impact on the customer service level in a company which places a node of the sales automation system in the manufacturing area. Manufacturing and inventory managers view the sales pipeline, continuously analyze the forecasted product mix by opportunity, follow and assess probabilities, and plan inventories and manufacturing capabilities accordingly. The potential service improvements and cost savings (in production, inventory costs, utilization, and the like) ripple through the organization.

3. Competitive Intelligence.

The impact of a competitor's sales and marketing efforts is at least partially a measure of how long it takes a company to respond to it effectively. If it takes weeks or months to identify, quantify, and assess the potential effect of the competition's moves, enormous damage can be done. By the same token, emotionally overresponding to what is, in effect, a nonexistent threat can be an equally major mistake. Sales automation can provide real-time competitive tracking and analysis, which can effectively address these issues and communicate them to both sales and corporate marketing.

4. Team Selling and Customer Satisfaction.

In this world of "added-value" selling, customers' expectations of service and responsiveness continue to increase. They also expect their vendors to be organized and coordinated in their efforts. In other words, the service or administrative person who contacts an account is expected to be as familiar with that account as the salesperson who handles it (and vice versa!). Have you ever heard a customer say, "Don't your people ever talk to one another?" Their expectations are equally high when a new salesperson takes over their account. Customers are no longer as willing as they once were to keep retraining vendor sales reps. Instead, they expect the new sales rep to be fully up-to-date and maintain a seamless transfer.

We know that the technology of SFA and communications software is in place so that the SFA customer database can be accessible and shared by everyone who needs it — if the salesperson is willing to be responsible for ensuring its completeness and accuracy!

> **MYTH: Sales automation will make salespeople
> more productive and more effective.
> REALITY: It's up to the salesperson!**

So the myth is that sales automation will make salespeople more productive and more effective! The reality is that it might, if it is used in the right way.

What we need is a workable and functional definition of SFA:

> ***Sales automation* is a "bridge" or "framework"
> that delivers information
> when, where, and to whom it's needed
> so that *better sales decisions* can be made
> to create a *competitive advantage*
> across the enterprise!**

Delivers Information.

That's it! SFA is an "information mover"; that's all it does. Its technology has the capability to deliver information almost immediately to whoever needs it wherever he or she may be.

Make Better Sales Decisions.

There is only one purpose for having information delivered — so that it can be used to help us create the best possible sales strategies and tactics that will give us the best potential of achieving our goals. In other words, better decisions create a new source of **competitive advantage**.

The key to achieving all the benefits of sales automation then comes down to **individual**

motivation. In other words, if we as a company provide the salespeople with the tools and the information that can enable them to make better sales decisions and become more competitive, the salespeople must be willing to make the necessary effort to use them. Make no mistake. It takes work and concentration and pure effort to plan and analyze the information recorded and provided in SFA — even if the work becomes easier than it might have been before. Logically, we would say, "Of course the reps will use it. They'll do anything if they can see it will make them more money!" (And that's a myth in its own right!)

Here is the net reality:

> **Sales automation will improve the productivity and effectiveness of salespeople who *want* to improve themselves and are willing to make the necessary investment in their personal success! Not everyone is willing to make that investment!**

The fact is that we would like to think of all salespeople as highly motivated because they have the potential to make incomes often far in excess of those in salaried positions. But as any sales manager knows, "It just ain't always so!" So "selling the reps" by attempting to show them how much more money they can potentially make does not always work! In other words, to motivate the salespeople we are going to need to develop multiple motivational strategies.

> **MYTH: Sales automation is for salespeople!**
> **REALITY: Sales automation is for everyone who makes sales decisions!**

Who makes sales decisions? Clearly, salespeople do. Sales managers are also pretty obvious. There are many people across the enterprise who make decisions, who rely on (or need) sales data, and who affect the ability of the salespeople to sell. Marketing is a clear example, but what about manufacturing, distribution, or product development? What about service and support, or even administrative staff in contracts or accounts receivable? Top management? Corporate planners and strategists? *Poor corporate decisions made more by gut feelings than by solid information hinder the salespeople's ability to sell!*

The concept was best expressed by a sales executive at a major computer manufacturer who described an issue he called *corporate disconnect*. Addressing his sales force, he explained it this way:

> We are facing a critical issue today that impacts not only the success of each of us and our company; it impacts our very survival! We call it "corporate disconnect." The problem is that, at corporate, there are three questions we can't answer:

1. **Who are our customers?** At corporate we have files and computers that give us "company names"; you in the field, however, know "who" the customers are — the relationships, opinions, needs, future plans, and so on.

2. **Why do they buy from us?** You in the field know the answers to this. At corporate we know only what we can pick up from call reports, surveys, or from what you tell us through your managers.

3. **Why do they quit buying?** And this is the critical question we need answers to — and don't have them. Why do we win; why do we lose? Why does a customer become dissatisfied?

This executive then posed a question that should be considered the quintessential question *and justification* of sales force automation:

> **"Without these answers, how can you in the field expect**
> **us at corporate to deliver to you**
> **the right products,**
> **at the right time**
> **with the right marketing**
> **and at the right price**
> **to provide you real competitive advantage?"**

The future holds a new **Corporate Information Highway** to help create smarter, more competitive companies.

FIGURE 1.4. THE CORPORATE INFORMATION HIGHWAY MODEL

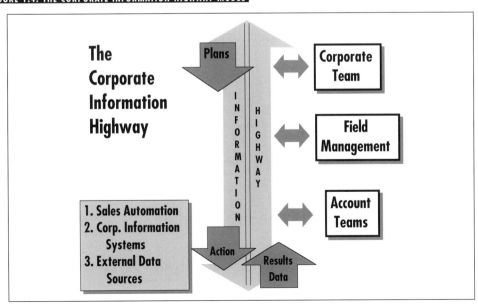

The *Corporate Information Highway* model is based on a data communications infrastructure throughout the corporate organization, logically linking people and departments who need to share information and work together more effectively. The technology is available today with products such as Lotus™ Notes, e-mail systems, and so on.

On that "highway" will be data from corporate's information systems (accounting, manufacturing, distribution, administration), as well as "groupware" applications such as e-mail, shared word processing, project development, price and product data, electronic presentations, and so on. External data sources will be more available with local and on-line links to data and information providers. Finally, using sales automation technology as the critical infrastructure, more accurate, complete, and real-time sales data will immediately be available across the corporation *to the people who need it, when they need it, and where they need it in order to make better sales decisions!*

How real is this model? Accomplishing it today to any extent can clearly be viewed as a potential source of competitive advantage. So a company asks itself, "Is this what we should focus on right now, or are there other more immediate needs?"

Establishing a corporate information highway today as an "early adopter" (with all the cultural and organizational changes that it implies) could be a real competitive advantage because it is still so new and its real potential still unrecognized. As the saying goes, "In the land of the blind, the one-eyed man is king!"

Consider, however, the potential cost of *not* doing it or *not* beginning active planning for it today. The Corporate Information Highway will *enable the corporation to follow the customer, not competition*. The corporation will be significantly better able to respond in real-time to customer needs and issues, trends, market events, and competitive intrusion—*delivering better products, at the right time, at the right price, with the right marketing!* This is a quantum leap in competitive advantage that may well become the norm in the next five years (or even less). **Those who are left behind may simply never catch up.**

An analogy from the earlier years of the computer industry may illustrate the corporate impact of technology's "paradigm shifts." In the early 1970s, as a young IBM marketing representative (sales rep), I sold business computers to $10–$20 million companies. At that time, many companies of that size relied on manual bookkeeping or "electronic ledger card machines" to manage their accounting functions. Business computers were still considered "leading edge."

As a young, aggressive sales rep, I would present to company presidents what I believed was an absolutely compelling argument for the incredible capability of IBM computers to improve their operations. We could help them better manage finances, reduce personnel costs, and in general improve their companies and make them more competitive—all *fully cost-justified!* More often than not, however, I was frustrated by executives who were content to keep things just the way they were, even in the face of enormous potential benefits. Naturally I rationalized that these presidents just didn't "get it" and were destined for business failure.

What took me twenty years to realize was that those executives *were not wrong*! In the business climate of the early seventies, manual or semi-automated accounting systems were fine *because that's what everyone used*! And then the paradigm changed. In the 1990s, no business of any size could compete without computerized financial management—if only because their bankers and investors would be appalled!

Sales automation's inevitability, in one form or another, is clear. It is also clear that at this moment in time, SFA is probably not a necessity to stay in business—yet. The corporate and management question is how long do we dare wait? Should we view SFA as a potential source of competitive advantage today or as a "stay-even" necessity later?

I attended a presentation by Jeremy Davis, formerly president of a Dun and Bradstreet company, who succinctly described the future's competitive environment: "If you're going to fail, fail fast, fix it, and get on with business!"

> **The measure of success is *not* if you are right all the time. No one ever is. Being "right" is at best an informed guess.**
>
> **Success is how quickly you find out you were wrong, how rapidly you can determine what was wrong, and how fast you can do something about it!**

> **MYTH: Sales automation will replace all the manual organizers and notetaking!**
> **REALITY: Salespeople will use both!**

The next myth is that you'll never need anything other than your sales automation system. In other words, sales automation will replace all the manual organizers and paper-based notetaking tools and replace it with electronic notetaking, electronic calendars, and so on. This is also called the *Dump the Paper Organizer*! myth. It's an attractive idea to further justify the system. Maybe someday, but not now.

The reality is that nobody is throwing away their organizers. The facts are that, if you are a remote (on the road) salesperson, computerized calendar and notetaking applications are virtually impractical. For example:

Customer: *"Are you free next Thursday for a meeting?"*

Salesperson: *"Just a minute, let me unpack my computer and boot it up; shouldn't take more than a few minutes ... whoops! Low battery! Do you mind if I crawl under your desk to plug this thing in?"*

Actually this isn't a problem with SFA software or its capability. "Instant-on" hardware capabilities could change this significantly, although they are not widely available yet.

Another reality is that the computer gets heavy! Yes, notebook computers have become significantly smaller and lighter than they were just a few years ago; battery life is longer, and so on. But as any outside salesperson knows—especially those of us who run through airports—by the time you add extra batteries and a charger, and pack everything else in the case, that thing gets a little bit heavy.

So what's the reality of how we use SFA systems today? Salespeople take paper notes during sales calls and manage their paper-based calendars in real-time. They update their SFA records *after the fact*; some right after the call, some at the end of the day, and some at night at home or in a hotel room. Yes, it takes longer; yes, it is duplication; and yes, it is valuable because it creates a comprehensive data file of account information that can be used as a tool for developing better strategies and tactics.

A note on the future: A viable solution to resolving the hardware usability issues might eventually be found in the PDAs (personal digital assistant) such as Apple Computer's "Newton" or Hewlett-Packard's "Omni-Go," or others. The PDAs are rapidly becoming more powerful but, in my opinion, we are still quite a way off from replacing the notebook computer (if only because there are many times a rep needs full keyboard capability). An intriguing model, however, packages the PDA with the notebook computer as an integrated system. Local and remote communication links between the two (and then on to corporate) will allow a salesperson to easily carry, access, and *enter* key opportunity, contact, and activity information—regularly updated to and from the rep's notebook computer—on the PDA. In this scenario, "pen technology" notetaking with handwriting recognition could make SFA a more practical real-time tool for the salesperson. We'll have to see.

> **MYTH: The field of dreams: If you build it they will come!**
> **REALITY: Salespeople will use SFA when they perceive**
> **a return on their investment!**

Quoting from the Kevin Costner movie *Field of Dreams*, "If you build it they will come." In other words, the myth is that if we can ever build a really good sales automation system that the reps really like, then they will welcome it with open arms and use it fully. This of course justifies why reps don't or won't use SFA, or quit using it: It just wasn't good enough; it has a bad "user interface"; and the like. It also sets up an impossible requirement—one product loved by everyone.

One reality is that there are many fine SFA packages on the market today, any number of which can undoubtedly fill almost any customer's requirements to solve business issues. And all are quite usable. The most important reality is that *salespeople will use SFA when they perceive a realistic return on investment*!

So how do we assure that salespeople get that return on investment—and where will it come from?

FIGURE 1.5. THE SALES RETURN-ON-INVESTMENT (ROI) MODEL

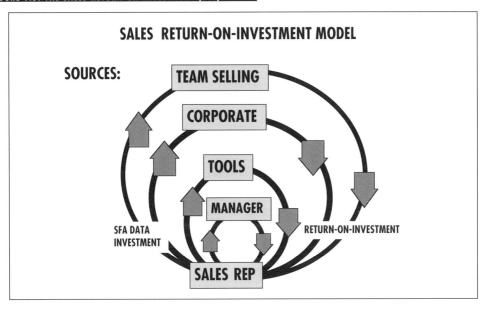

By implementing sales automation technology, we are asking salespeople and their managers to make two kinds of *investments*.

The first is **learning to do things differently**. This isn't just learning how to operate computers and software. That's relatively easy. The real task is learning new ways to manage our sales businesses. This is even more difficult when people don't perceive anything fundamentally wrong with the way they do things now. There is an initial "honeymoon period" during which trying out the new technologies is fun, but there comes a point when we all *hit the wall*! That is, in the pressure and hurry-up real world of selling, we find ourselves "called" back to old techniques and tools which are more comfortable and seem faster than the new methods (even if logically they are less effective). Psychologists tell us this is a consistent model of human behavior that when new ways of doing things (behaviors) are introduced, 80% of the people will go back to their old, more comfortable ways within twelve months if they receive no other reinforcement. It *will* take an investment of time and effort before the salespeople feel the new methods are faster or have proof that they are more effective.

FIGURE 1.6. BEHAVIOR RATE OF EXTINCTION MODEL

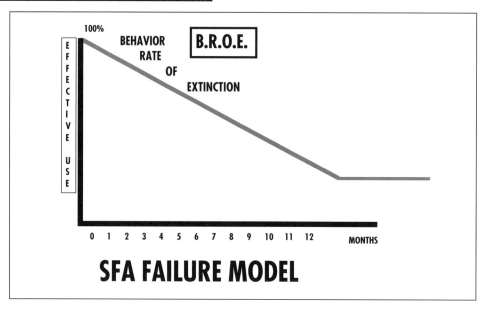

The second investment is **data**. We are asking the salespeople to make an investment of *additional* time and effort (particularly early on when it's most difficult) to enter *comparatively* large amounts of accurate and complete data on account, opportunity, and activity — and do so every day.

On top of all this, the salespeople still have to "make their numbers." There needs to be a pretty fair ROI somewhere here to make SFA or any new system happen.

Overall, there are four possible sources of return on investment to the salespeople, but how and when they can be achieved needs to play an important role in our overall strategy and expectations for success.

FIGURE 1.7. FIRST ROI: SALES TOOLS

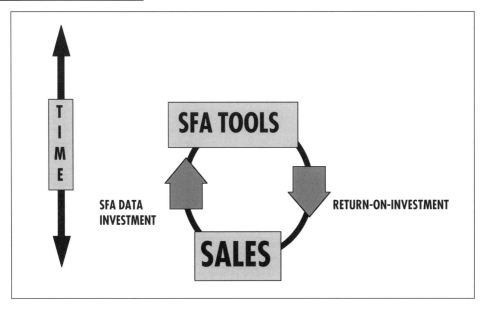

Assumption:

We can logically show salespeople how once they have achieved a high competency level, the "sales tools" in automation systems will clearly benefit them. Tracking activities and "to-do's," data analysis, lead management, opportunity management—they all make logical sense. We should expect to see immediate results!

Truth:

It will take three to nine months before a salesperson recognizes any improvement in personal productivity or effectiveness! The time differential is a factor of many things—computer literacy, experience, attitude, and ability to handle change, or speed of learning. In that period, however, how many will give up at least partially and return to the old ways of doing things? Once we lose them, it will be twice as hard to get them back.

FIGURE 1.8. SECOND ROI: TEAM SELLING

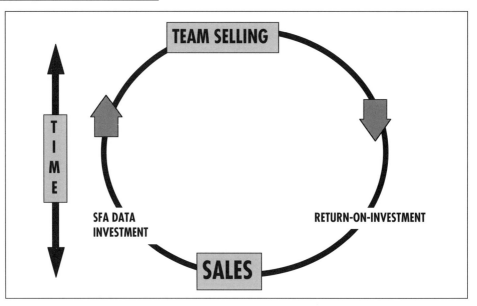

We've generally discussed what can happen when everyone across the sales enterprise is working together through sales automation. This is team selling, although a simpler version is just the linking of field personnel who directly work with the customer.

Assumption:

Through SFA everyone on the "sales or account team" can be kept up to date on activities, sales plans and strategies, personnel changes, sales progress, relationships, and so on. Companies that have implemented SFA-based team selling recognize it as an exceptionally high-value application. We should expect team selling to be an early benefit of sales force automation!

Truth:

From the beginning of the SFA project, team selling can take from two to three years to achieve. Why so long? Most SFA projects begin with a pilot and, later in the first year, progress to a roll-out of just the sales force and managers. Now not only must the salespeople go through a learning curve, but also the SFA system must be tuned and modified until a stable database is achieved. Support personnel usually come on-line after this and must address their own learning curve and tuning process. Finally, all organizations must learn new ways of working together. It's going to take a while.

FIGURE 1.9. THIRD ROI: A SMARTER COMPANY

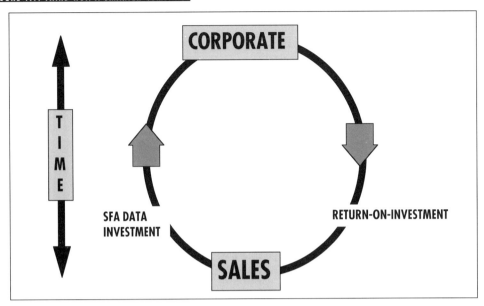

Assumption:

A company that solves the "corporate disconnect" problem and begins to construct a "Corporate Information Highway" becomes a smarter company that can better support its salespeople. As data start coming in, we will see an improvement in our marketing focus, management effectiveness, and corporate planning and direction, resulting in greater competitive advantage for the salespeople!

Truth:

The company won't be visibly or appreciably smarter for at least one year! Assume that from day one, the company begins collecting and sharing sales and progress data which are highly accurate and complete. (That's a big assumption.) Even in the best case it will take a year to collect a *critical mass* of data sufficient to make decisions that are significantly more reliable than those made in the past.

We would hope that after one year the company is *smarter*, after two years it approaches *brilliance*, and after three it attains new levels of *genius*, but it's going to take a while.

So with all the potential of sales tools, team selling, and a smarter company, if the salespeople quit using the system in the first year—or even use it partially so that the data that is collected becomes inaccurate and incomplete—*little or no benefit will ever be recognized by anyone!*

FIGURE 1.10. FOURTH ROI: THE SALES MANAGER

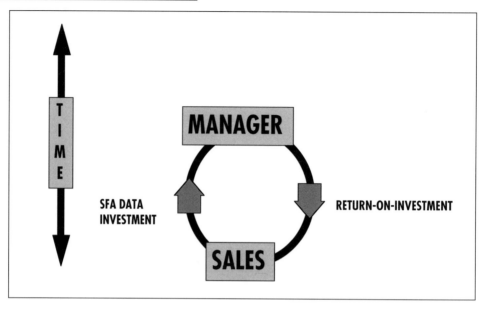

Fact:

Sales organizations ignore sales managers in sales automation (and implementing new sales methodologies) and consider SFA only a tool for the salespeople.

Truth:

Of all the potential sources of return-on-investment to the salesperson, only the sales manager has the ability to provide ROI from day one through coaching. When SFA becomes the fundamental tool for management coaching—that is, sales managers *require* sales reps to utilize the sales automation system as a strategic planner (not just a data collector!) for every active opportunity and then coach to this—then sales reps *will* use SFA. Why? For a couple of reasons: first, because it is required of them; and second, because they can receive immediate and valuable coaching assistance that quickly translates into more successful sales.

In fact, to make sales automation "easy" at the start, managers need only *require* the salespeople to do three things with SFA:

1. Keep company, opportunity, and contact profile data up-to-date and accurate.
2. Log *major* activities. Don't bother with "left message" and the like unless they want to.
3. Plan and log *what they plan to do next* for each active opportunity.

There's much more to most sales automation systems, and some people will use more of the capabilities than others from the start. But as we will see throughout this book, these three minimum requirements are what we really need to find and realize SFA success.

Experience has shown that if we can maintain 100% usage and a high quality of data *for one year* with salespeople, not only will SFA become a permanent part of the corporate culture, but also we will at least begin to recognize the corporate, team selling, and sales tool benefits.

THE FINAL REALITY

No one has ever solved a sales problem by throwing software at it or ever will!

This is perhaps as good an axiom as any other to begin with. In other words, to realize automation success, sales and marketing organizations will have to go *beyond sales automation* as a computer application to a total reassessment of what selling is and what we want it to be as we enter the third millennium.

CHAPTER 2

THE SALES MANAGER/ SALES AUTOMATION EQUATION

MIDNIGHT MADNESS OR "IT'S 12:00 A.M. YOU'RE WIDE AWAKE!"

It's 12:00 A.M. and the sales manager is wide awake. The end of the month (quarter, year) is coming up, and he or she is having a midnight attack of the FUDS (fears, uncertainties, and doubts). "Will we make the numbers? How reliable is the forecast? Is there enough business in the pipeline? How confident do I feel? I'll call all my reps first thing in the morning, and we'll go over each deal again." (They'll appreciate that!)

There are sales management questions that have never had really good answers, the kind that wake you in the middle of the night and keep you that way. You try to get back to sleep. No luck. And so you go to the kitchen for a glass of water and a swig of Maalox. Another long night.

THE SEVEN ULCERS OF SALES MANAGEMENT

Ulcer 1: "What's going on out there?"

Perhaps because most sales managers were first successful salespeople, they're used to being in control of events and staying on top of each sales situation. All that changes as a manager when you realize that the salespeople don't relish writing activity reports, educating you on each opportunity (especially daily), and answering "Did you..." questions ("Did you qualify that deal? Did you ask for the order?"). Wouldn't it be nice to find a way to know what's going on without "micromanaging" and driving the salespeople (and yourself) crazy?

Ulcer 2: "Where did all the leads go?"

Remember the 500 leads from that trade show? When you looked through the cards, there were some great "Call me ASAP!" opportunities. You know — well, you are pretty sure, anyway — that marketing sent the leads to your sales reps. Now it's been three months, and it seems like nothing's happened. Didn't the reps follow up? (You told them to at your team meeting!) Nobody seems to be able to give you a specific answer. It is a black hole!

Ulcer 3: "What are the reps up to?"

If the sales reps are in the office, you know what they're doing. It just isn't selling. On the other hand, when you haven't seen them for six weeks, well, you get a little nervous! Better leave voice mails for all the reps to call in ASAP!

Ulcer 4: "Are we going to make the numbers?"

The big question. Will we make it? How accurate is the forecast? You're trying to remember every deal that should close. Even though the rep said not to worry, how confident do you really feel? You remember how you used to forecast when you were a rep. Oh no! We're in real trouble now! The pressure's on from upstairs too!

Ulcer 5: "My best sales rep just quit!"

If you're really lucky, he or she just retired to the Bahamas. If you're really unlucky, that rep now works for the competition and is coming after his or her old customers. To make it worse, the new salesperson you assigned says that she can't find any files to speak of, and nobody seems to know what "Best Rep" was working on or who the contacts were in the accounts. Oh boy!

Ulcer 6: "How can I help?"

And here's the bottom line, every manager's real question. You were probably a pretty good sales rep, even great! You love to sell, make calls, brainstorm, and set strategies. Trouble is, there's no time. The sales reps don't invite you on calls as much as you'd like, and when you do go you find it's hard to really help "make it happen" because you're not as close to the account as the sales rep. (Another "schmooze" call.) Rats!

Ulcer 7: "If we're so busy, why am I worried?"

The most unsettling question of all makes you doubt your sanity. Everyone is moving ahead quickly, but still you're left with the nagging suspicion that there's no plan, no strategy. You don't know where you're going, but you're confident that you're making good time!

We really need a cure for "Midnight Madness!"

The fundamental and most basic job of a sales manager is to maximize sales performance. That's a simple statement for one of the most difficult jobs in the world of business. It makes little difference if the economy is booming or in a recession, or whether the company currently has competitive advantage or disadvantage in the marketplace The sales manager will be judged on his or her ability to direct, coach, and motivate salespeople to produce the necessary volume of bottom-line, profitable sales. As a result, every sales manager is always looking for ways to improve the overall effectiveness of the salespeople, and for tools to improve his or her personal ability to have an impact on sales performance.

THE SALES MANAGER EQUATION:
METHODOLOGY + TECHNOLOGY

This year sales managers and their companies will spend millions of dollars in the effort to relieve "Midnight Madness." That investment will run the gamut from sales training in sales skills to sophisticated sales strategy methodologies for "opportunity management," to advanced sales automation technology — equipping field salespeople with sophisticated computer systems that run state-of-the-art software sales tools, such as electronic mail, contact and opportunity management systems, access to on-line marketing databases, and much more.

FIGURE 2.1. INTEGRATION OF METHODOLOGY AND TECHNOLOGY

The **Critical Future of Sales Automation**
PROCESS INTEGRATION

Selling Methodology

+

Sales Automation

Better Sales Strategies and Tactics

Maximum Results Execution

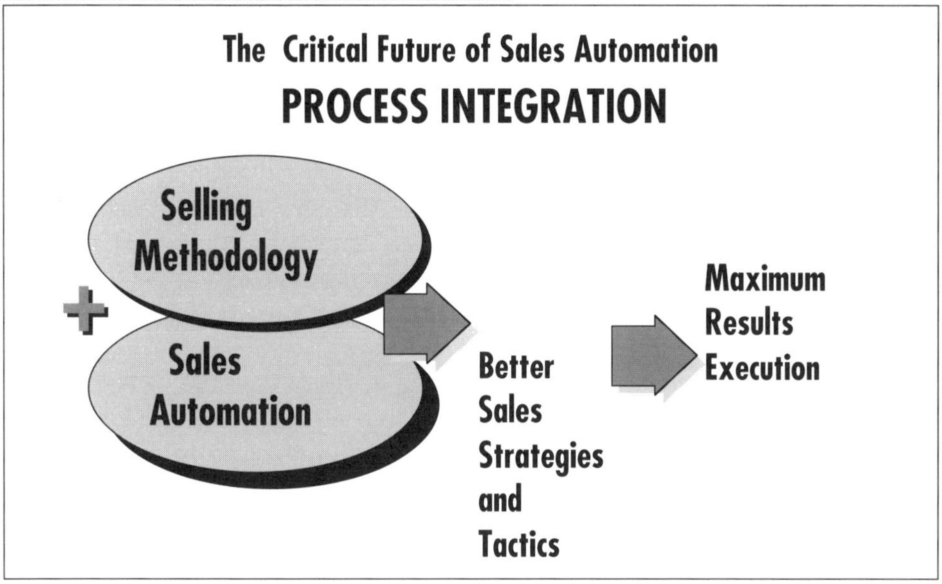

The combination of **opportunity management methodology** and **sales automation technology** is the powerful, new tool kit for sales managers (and their people) that can effectively leverage sales performance in ways never before dreamed of — and solve "Midnight Madness." What is this remarkable combination? Simply put, *opportunity management methodologies* are sales planning and analysis systems that help managers and salespeople assess and determine the most effective strategies and tactics to win business. *Sales automation technology* provides the "enabling tools" to assure that salespeople can carry out those strategies and tactics as productively and efficiently as possible. Methodology and technology, however, are a package. They go together, and they are absolutely dependent upon each other to achieve the fullest success! When the two are integrated and combined, both sales and management have an exciting new set of capabilities that can have a measurable and significant impact in the selling marketplace.

Many managers know the experience of training and retraining the sales force in opportunity management or other planning and selling skills and being expected to assure that the reps use and follow them. Unfortunately, that has too often turned out to be a cumbersome task at best — with reams of paper forms to be filled out and mailed back and forth and with time delays that limit how useful the methods can be in the real world of selling. Over time, many reps quit using the methods or only use pieces rather than the full program. When used at all, the methods often become just another form of sales *tracking*, not sales *planning*, and they are not especially helpful as a coaching tool.

Technology, in the form of sales automation, has had much the same problem. The idea behind it was that if salespeople were provided with comprehensive account and territory information electronically, and if they kept more detailed and organized activity records in a database and made use of on-line tools to manage their calendar, mail, and proposals, then they would make better sales decisions, execute them better, and make better use of their time. For example, automation should enable quicker response to customer requests, better follow-up, less time spent reporting, and generally a more focused, planned sales effort. And managers have been told to make sure the salespeople used the technology.

Some salespeople, however, have never been fully convinced that they really *needed* the detailed information or the electronic organization tools in automation technology to do their jobs effectively, nor were they completely sure what they were supposed to do differently with all that technology. So, like methodology, many sales automation systems have been used in pieces and have evolved into sales tracking systems, not the comprehensive sales process systems they were expected to be.

Despite these problems, almost everyone still agrees that both sales methodology training and sales automation are potentially worthwhile. Sales organizations *do* get returns on their investments even when the new skills and automation systems are used only partially. But there's also a common lament that there is still a real potential for even greater results *if only everyone would use them like they're supposed to!*

The good news is that there is a solution. Opportunity management methodology and sales automation technology, when they are integrated and used together, are the resolution for each other's fundamental problems. Designed and implemented together and used in a common sales program, they can accomplish the following:

1. Realize the potential of each to become a tool for sales planning and improving sales focus.
2. Provide a new and powerful, real-time coaching tool for sales managers.
3. Achieve 100% usage of *both* among the sales force.

The key seems to be in the realization that methodology and technology support and drive the usage of each other!

From one perspective, *sales automation* provides a way to support and enhance *opportunity management*

1. by providing and organizing customer and market information so that salespeople can easily use it as part of their sales planning and process tracking (the methodology)
2. by eliminating cumbersome paper forms and replacing them with electronic screens
3. by providing a real-time communication link to sales management for joint development of sales strategy and post-call debriefing.

Methodology, conversely, provides a way to support and enhance the use of sales automation

1. by answering the questions "Why am I entering all this information?" and "How do I use it?"
2. by providing a "strategic framework" for sales and management to discuss sales progress and plan jointly, not just review past sales activity.

The methodology/technology investment also adds a new wrinkle to the sales manager's job. Not only must the manager produce sales results, but also he or she ultimately becomes responsible for assuring that the combination of sales methodologies and automation technology pays for itself, that is, produces even greater sales volumes and profits. In short, a key new management task will be to make sure that each sales rep not only uses this sales system competently, but also applies it as an *effective* sales tool. This is fine if you know how.

The problem is that as sales managers, many of us are little more knowledgeable about this new "selling with technology" business than our salespeople are and perhaps even less knowledgeable than others. The more recent college graduates are computer-literate, and they expect (demand?) to use computer systems as fundamental business tools. On the other hand, many of our more experienced salespeople may not yet be fully comfortable with technology and may even resist it. It gets worse the farther up the corporate ladder we go.

Times have really changed. It used to be that, by definition, a manager was someone who was experienced and successful in every aspect of the salesperson's job. He or she could, therefore, reliably be counted on to provide the right advice and direction, based on personal experience if nothing else. But today, at least as far as sales technology goes, we're all learning together and wondering sometimes if there are more questions than answers.

So the question is, *exactly* what is the best way for salespeople and their managers to use this new combination of opportunity management methodology and sales automation technology? Are computerized sales tools really better than traditional paper forms, organizers, and filing systems? Where's the payoff?

To answer these questions, we need to start with a closer look at the *business* of selling and what salespeople need in order to be competitive in today's marketplace.

THE BUSINESS OF SELLING: OLD YANKEES AND SLED DOGS

In my home of New Hampshire, there are more than a few "old Yankees" around, and there's still a bit of "old Yankee wisdom" floating about. For example, my neighbor, Oren, usually has a comment or two on most things in life. If you ask him how deep the snow was last year, it was about "chest high on a duck, ayuh." (There's still a lot of Yankee wisdom I haven't figured out yet.) Nonetheless, some of what he has to say is occasionally relevant to the business of selling.

Once, Oren asked me if I "was any good" at selling. I said (with appropriate modesty, of course) that I thought so.

"Well, just you remembah," said Oren, **"if you ain't the lead sled dog the view never changes."**

Like a lot of Oren's "wisdom," I didn't give it much thought at first, but later I think that "the lead sled dog" is really about developing **competitive advantage**.

Selling is fundamentally the business of establishing competitive advantage in order to win. A sale can only be made when the salesperson has established unique competitive advantage in the mind of the buyer. Of all the competitors, only one salesperson will be able to do that for each "deal"—and that's the lead sled dog.

> **First Axiom of Selling:**
> **A sale is made when the salesperson establishes**
> **a unique competitive advantage in the mind of the buyer.**

We first need to understand sales automation and opportunity management in terms of how, together, they can help salespeople establish that unique competitive advantage. Why? Because if they can't do that, then there's no reason to go any further.

What is *competitive advantage*? Salespeople sometimes think of competitive advantage in terms of only product advantage or price advantage. The fact is that generally speaking, sales automation can't do a great deal to impact either of these. So, not surprisingly, many sales reps won't necessarily view automation as an important part of their competitive strategy. However, the problem with advantage based solely on either product or price is that both are temporary. A competitor's new product announcement or pricing strategy can wipe out advantage overnight. What's more, *neither of these has a great deal to do with nor is really under the control of the salesperson.*

Every salesperson has to bring something else to the table, something that, despite the relative advantages or disadvantages of price or product, successfully leverages the "buy decision" of the customer. In a very real sense then, the competitive advantage the sales rep brings to the sale can only be the salesperson him or herself—with three critical characteristics:

1. **Self.** Someone the customer wants to do business with, and who has a positive attitude and an interest in the customer's needs and success.
2. **Unique Value.** Someone who brings a special expertise in or knowledge of a product, industry, application, or the customer's business to the sale and can establish a high level of perceived value in the mind of the customer.
3. **Execution.** Someone who possesses solid interpersonal selling skills combined with business planning and tactical skills and who can put them together to close the sale as quickly and efficiently as possible.

It is in these last two, Unique Value and Execution, that the combination of methodology and sales automation can be a powerful tool for leveraging competitive advantage.

THE SUCCESS EQUATION

Second Axiom of Selling:
Sales Success = Quality x Execution

Success in selling—the ability of a salesperson to successfully establish unique competitive advantage—can be expressed in the Success Equation: Sales Success equals Quality times Execution.

Quality can be defined as figuring out the *best* things to do (strategies and tactics) that will most effectively advance the sales effort. For example:
- Selecting the highest potential opportunities
- Correctly assessing the investment necessary to win
- Making the right calls on the right people at the right time with the right message
- Assessing competitive position
- Having the right information and knowledge about customer needs
- Knowing how to work through the customer's decision-making processes
- Defining and delivering what constitutes real value to the customer.

In short, *quality* is developing the optimal sales strategies and in general making the best possible decisions on how to pursue the opportunity most effectively (and sometimes when not to pursue!).

Execution is how well we can carry out the strategy — the *delivery* of the plan. If *execution* is our ability to make great sales calls, then *quality* is determining which great calls to make!

How important are these two elements? Do the math in the following example:

Step 1: Let's start with a high-quality idea or strategy for a specific sales call. It's clearly the right thing to do, so we'll score it a 10 out of 10.

Step 2: Unfortunately, because of incomplete knowledge or weak sales skills, the call is executed poorly. Score 0 out of 10.

Step 3: If $Q \times E$ = Success, then our equation is $10 \times 0 = 0$.

Result: A really good idea executed poorly brings predictable results. No sale.

Of course, the equation works the other way as well. A really bad idea ($Q = 0$) that is incredibly well executed ($E = 10$) still results in a success score of 0. No sale!

The objective is to assure the highest quality strategies and planned tactics (all tens!) and execute them flawlessly: $10 \times 10 = 100$ = Success!

SALES AUTOMATION — A 180-DEGREE ROTATION

Salespeople too often look at sales automation as a database into which they are supposed to enter sales data and activity information for the company and their managers. In this age of corporate layoffs and downsizing they may tend to see it as a tracking system developed by the company to make sure they are making a required number of calls, in other words, to check that they are not "goofing off." Admittedly, some sales managers do in fact view automation as a tool to enable undreamed of levels of micromanagement. So, when the salespeople are told that the real purpose of entering all that data is to make them more productive and efficient than before, well, a little skepticism is to be expected.

It's time to do a 180-degree rotation in our thinking about sales automation. Looking "backward" (tracking) is fine; it can help us identify trends and understand what worked, what didn't, and why. But computerized tracking systems are not going to develop the kind of sales advantage we're talking about here. The payoff will be in looking "forward," in viewing sales automation as a tool to help salespeople and managers *jointly* plan for maximum quality and execution, the tools of competitive advantage.

Another element of this new sales automation view is a corporate perspective called "Who's following whom?" or "The Pied Piper lives!"

Flying between Boston and San Francisco not long ago, thumbing through one of the airline magazines, I came across an article that caught my attention. It suggested that more than 90% of all sales and marketing decisions are based on only one factor: *what the competition is doing*! It occurs to me that perhaps the Pied Piper is alive and well in "Businesstown," but where is he taking us?

Here's a common marketing scenario. One company cleverly comes out with a new product feature or service which they believe will give them competitive advantage, or perhaps they announce a new pricing strategy or a sale or a new marketing program or promotion. As we said before, this kind of advantage is temporary at best, and it won't be long before everyone else responds by following this new Pied Piper. Examples abound everywhere. Look at the major long-distance telephone services. In jockeying for market position, they have created the most confusing set of products and services in the history of business (at least I can't figure out all the plans and special "deals"!). The airline price wars are another example. One cuts prices and the others follow. Likewise, personal computers are in a constant battle for feature and price advantage. This scenario is played out in just about every industry.

Since we're all following the competition, we better hope that they know what they're doing better than we do. The Pied Piper is alive and well, but remember what happened to the rats!

It occurs to me that the "leaders" we *need* to be following are not our competitors but our *customers and prospects*. If we were able to listen and accurately interpret what they're saying—and understand what they really need—then we could be assured that we're on course to develop real competitive advantage.

> ## Third Axiom of Selling:
> ## Follow the Customer!

The problem is that finding out what the customers are saying and thinking is perhaps the most difficult task in business. However, the fact is that, generally speaking, our *salespeople* do know the answers—and they do want to tell us. Unfortunately, collecting and transmitting that information to our marketing and product people who need it, in a reliable, real-time format from which high-probability decisions can be made, has proven to be almost an impossibility. (Which is, of course, why we follow the competition in the beginning. If they're doing something and their sales *appear* to be increasing, they might be more reliable than our own information or "best guesses.")

If there is an overwhelming justification for sales automation, it is this: *Sales automation can create a real-time information link from the customers, through our salespeople, direct to the corporate planning rooms*, and that will be worth more than all the "pied pipers" in the marketplace. The result will be a mix of the highest-quality plans and strategies executed perfectly to drive more business than ever before.

As one CEO told me, "I'm sick of following the competition. For once I'd like to be the one the competition follows!"

Given this new perspective on the purpose of technology, let's revise our definition of sales automation:

> **Sales automation is a framework for opportunity management (the development of strategies and tactics).**
>
> **SFA moves Information when, where, and to whom it's needed across the business enterprise to enable better *sales planning* to make better *sales decisions* that will create *competitive advantage*.**

So in addition to taking a new look at sales automation, we also have to do the same for opportunity management sales planning.

OPPORTUNITY MANAGEMENT SALES PLANNING — A 180-DEGREE ROTATION

Opportunity management is the combination of territory, account, and "deal" or opportunity planning. Every sales manager and rep knows they need them, but no one really wants to do them. Still, they are a critical element of the *sales success equation* ($S = Q \times E$) because they are the only way we can assure the "quality" factor of the sales effort. Account planning methodologies have proliferated in the training marketplace in recent years and, generally speaking, most professional sales organizations have invested in one or more. This is especially true of, but not limited to, organizations whose products and services are complex in nature or who sell to larger accounts with more complex buying processes.

Some training experts estimate that one year after training, less than 15% of those trained continue to actively utilize the methodology. If this is true, then either account planning is unnecessary or perhaps there is something fundamentally weak with such programs. The question is, "If we agree that effective opportunity management can in fact help salespeople close more business quicker, then why wouldn't every salesperson utilize it to the fullest?"

WHAT'S WRONG WITH PLANNING SYSTEMS?

A group of high-technology salespeople recently completed an annual two-day account-planning exercise. They were asked two questions: "Why do you plan?" and "What is the result of your planning?" Here were their typical responses:

- "The purpose of planning is to make you take time out and think about business."
- "It's a good exercise, but not very real-world because things change during the year."

- "Mostly it's for management. They get nervous without it!"
- "I don't know. I turn in my plan and never see it again."
- "Nobody expects you to *actually* follow the plan."
- "This technique is fine, but it's too complex with so many boxes to fill in!"
- "I could never remember to use all this on a day-to-day basis. And who's got the time anyway?"
- "I'm part of a sales team (sales, support, partners). What good is planning our accounts without them?"
- "Train, train, train! We need to be out selling, not sitting in class!"
- "We're supposed to figure out how to provide more added value. Whatever that is."

What do these responses tell us about the perceptions of planning by the sales force and by their management? Here are seven primary issues that need to be addressed to make planning work:

1. **Thinking Is Good.** Most salespeople agree that taking time to *think* about their accounts, review their goals, and refine their plans is a good idea. Few, however, feel that it is valuable enough for them to be taken out of the field for training or frequent planning sessions.

2. **Things Change.** The problem with annual account plans is that then tend to be *static*. In today's marketplace of constant re-engineering programs, downsizing, acquisition, and general reorganizations (both our own and our customer's), today's plan may be completely out of date in a month or less.

3. **Who's the Planning For?** Fairly or unfairly, planning systems are often regarded by salespeople more as a form of management audit than as a sales success tool. One sales rep who was asked at what times during the sales year he referred to his completed account plans, answered, "My manager keeps them. And if he pulls them out, I wonder if it means he's looking for a reason to fire me!"

   That is probably an extreme answer that was given somewhat tongue-in-cheek, but it serves to illustrate who the real "keeper of the plan" is — management, not the salesperson.

4. **Follow That Plan? How?** Account *planning* systems are too often just that — plans. Plans have little or no value unless they directly translate into sales *actions*. In other words, plans are *strategies*, and strategies without resultant *tactics* are useless!

5. **Brilliant Complexity.** Account planning systems training is a highly competitive marketplace, and developers strive to add new and "more powerful" features as a source of competitive advantage for their methodology. Unfortunately there are times when this results in planning systems of increased complexity. They are brilliant in concept and design but impossible to implement in the fast-paced world of selling.

6. **Planning in a Vacuum.** Team selling is an increasingly important trend in today's selling

environment. As the sales rep said, the effort is useless unless the entire team knows the planning methodology and participates. Many companies, however, limit opportunity management training to account managers and not their field or internal support personnel.

7. **Planning and Coaching Disconnect.** Many sales managers still track and evaluate sales progress by sales activity levels (for example, number of calls made per week). Few actively utilize sales plans as elements of their regular sales coaching. It is not surprising, then, that most salespeople consider their *overall activity level* to be more important to their success than the *efficiency or effectiveness* of their activities.

GUIDELINES FOR OPPORTUNITY MANAGEMENT PLANNING SUCCESS

The following guidelines should be used as the "rules of the road" in designing or selecting a sales planning system. No single system or methodology will, of course, be right for every sales organization, but all should conform to at least this set of simple principles.

1. **Planning Supports the Sales Process.** The only purpose of planning is to improve the quality and effectiveness of the salesperson's sales activities. In short, planning must *directly* help the salesperson determine the *most effective tactics or actions* that will most quickly advance him or her to the close. In other words, planning needs to be more than just an annual "thinking about the business" session.

2. **Planning Is Multitiered.** Planning systems must directly address the three basic modes or focuses of selling: account, opportunity, and contact. First, salespeople develop overall *territory* and *account* plans, goals, and general strategies. Second, salespeople develop specific *opportunity* plans to qualify, develop, and win "deals." Finally, salespeople develop individualized *contact* plans to obtain the support and agreement of the decision makers, influencers, and approvers who ultimately make the buy decision. A viable planning system must include each of these three elements.

3. **Planning Is a Team Sport.** Effective planning systems must lend themselves to the joint planning efforts of disparate team members who may include sales, pre- and post-sales support, marketing, and third-party sales partners.

4. **Planning Must Be Executable.** Simple does not necessarily mean ineffective. The result of planning must be a set of "executable" sales tactics or actions. So, beware of complexity for complexity's sake.

5. **Planning Must Be "Living."** "Living" plans do not end up in file cabinets. An initial training or planning session should only generate a first-step plan which will be and can be continuously modified and refined — even on a day-to-day basis — as the sales situation inevitably changes. (This is an important capability of sales automation.)

6. **Planning Is a Coaching Tool.** Effective planning systems should not be "gotcha" documents. They should facilitate a *joint planning dialogue* between the salesperson and the man-

ager and among the account team members to continually assess strategies, planned tactics, and opportunity viability as the opportunity progresses through the sales cycle.

7. **Planning Must Be Educationally Integrated.** Typically, salespeople receive training in a variety of subject areas: product, sales skills, and later management skills, account planning, and others. Effective opportunity management systems must be integrated with these related training areas and assure consistency of terms and concepts. This concept will be covered in detail in the "Strategy Mapping" section of this book.

8. **Planning and Training Must Be Marketing-Based.** By "marketing-based," we mean that planning systems must be able to take into account and support the corporate marketing strategy. The concepts of not only what a company sells but also how it plans to sell it must be clearly integrated into the system. At a minimum, this means that training case studies and other exercises should be market and company specific. At best, the planning training program should include a completed plan or strategy for a current, real-life account or sales opportunity.

9. **Planning Should Be Value-Based.** Professional outside sales is today, by and large, based upon added-value selling. Central to any planning methodology should be a focus on defining and providing what it is that provides unique value to the customers. Ultimately, value and its perception by the customer create the basis for all strategic and tactical thinking. More on this when we discuss creating "Value Products" as a new source of competitive advantage.

10. **Planning Must Be Technology Supportable.** Opportunity management must be fully integrated and supported by sales automation technology in order to develop high utilization and maximum possible results.

To put it all together then, sales are the result of competitive advantage which *must be created by the salesperson*. To do this successfully will require a focus by salespeople *and their managers* on developing the highest quality sales strategies, planning the best sales tactics, and executing them to perfection. Sales automation and opportunity management *used correctly and in tandem*, are the new tools to help us do both of these better. They are the "interlocking components" of the sales manager's tool kit.

SALES MANAGERS' PERSPECTIVES

THIRSTY HORSES — MORE CONVERSATIONS WITH OREN

I walked down the road to visit Oren again yesterday. Oren, "old Yankee" that he is, usually has some thoughts on the business of life that he'll share while sitting on the front porch on a summer night. I told him about a particularly frustrating sales situation with which I'd been involved. After a long sales cycle, during which the salesperson had apparently done everything "right" to an apparently enthusiastic buyer, the prospect just wouldn't close.

"Well," I said philosophically, "it just proves the old saying 'You can lead a horse to water, but you can't make him drink.'"

After a while Oren replied, "Well, seems t'me that somebody f'got t'ask the horse if'n he was thirsty before leadin' him all that way."

As usual, Oren cuts to the heart of the issue.

Sometimes in selling, it's easy to confuse a prospect's apparent willingness to look at our product with a real "thirst" for it. It's especially so when the prospect gives us continuing positive feedback or works with us through a long selling cycle. Despite how we may feel, the prospect usually hasn't been wasting our time; in most cases, he or she has been looking along the way for a solid business reason to buy, but never found it.

In other words, a prospect can want our product but not need it, and without a clear need—a real thirst—he or she will never close.

Successful salespeople and managers are experts in building excitement and enthusiasm for their products and services. Don't stop. But you might want to ask that horse a time or two if he's really thirsty before you get all the way down to the river.

CHAPTER 3

SALES METAMORPHOSIS — CHANGES IN THE FORM, FUNCTION, AND STRUCTURE OF SELLING AND MANAGING

The dictionary definition of *metamorphosis* is "a change in form, structure, or function as a result of development which is often more or less sudden." That's a particularly apt description of what is happening to the world of sales and sales management today. The *forms, structures,* and even the *functions* are changing dramatically.

This change or metamorphosis is also comparatively *sudden*. Consider that not much has really changed in selling and managing in the last fifty years. Certainly improvements in transportation and communication have enhanced both jobs, but fundamentally selling has still been selling and managing has been managing. In other words, things have been done in much the same way they always have.

Beginning in the early 1990s, however, the game really changed. The advent of sales automation and other new technologies, combined with new theories of corporate re-engineering, is rapidly redefining the role and even the purpose of outside salespeople and their managers. This continues to be an ongoing process that is gathering momentum. The problem is that these new roles and corporate expectations are fluid; that is, they are still being defined and are changing almost daily, and there is a lot of experimentation going on. But above all things, change is certain!

Sales managers and their salespeople need to take an active role in helping to define, direct, and even enable this process of sales metamorphosis, or risk becoming its victim. The challenge is to understand why this change is happening, the market pressures that are driving it, the potential outcomes, and how to find selling success in the midst of it.

SALES MANAGEMENT REVEILLE — THE WAKE-UP CALL

Here's an interesting question. Do we really need first-line sales managers anymore? There have been a number of recent articles in national magazines posing this very question. More than one "re-engineering theorist" has suggested that as companies "re-engineer" their sales and marketing organizations, most sales managers will be eliminated. They see future field salespeople *empowered* as "microbusinesses" through technology. In short, traditional salespeople, as employees utilizing *virtual office* technology, might work as functionally independent small businesses. Technology, not managers, could enable corporations to communicate with salespeople and accurately track and analyze sales progress. A realistic estimate is that for every five managers today only one will be needed in the not-too-distant future.

To the accountants this is perhaps an attractive proposition. Using the technology of sales force automation, sales organizations are already closing expensive remote offices and reducing expensive administrative personnel overhead — with reported bottom-line impact of up to 20%. Imagine how much more could be saved if they eliminate 80% of the sales managers as well. There's a terrifying thought for most sales managers!

The critical issue is that if the definition of sales manager is someone who *primarily* tracks and manages sales activity, forecasts sales revenues, and does general sales personnel admin-istration, then a valid case can probably be made that far fewer "managers" will soon be nec-essary. That translates to a *significant* potential reduction in sales overhead dollars and a real increase in selling margins. And make no mistake, in today's marketplace *margins* are what it's all about.

Few experienced sales managers would want to describe their roles this way or would want their jobs to go away. Most would admit, however, that too much time is, in fact, taken up with "administrivia" and not enough time is available for coaching and motivating the sales force.

I've asked hundreds of front-line sales managers to identify and prioritize what they consider to be their most important management tasks and roles. On their lists, coaching and motivating are always at the top, while activity tracking and administration invariably bring up the rear. Most managers do feel that their most important job is to play a significant and necessary role in the sales process, albeit one with more than a few frustrations and headaches. The corporation, however, often takes exactly the reverse view; first-line manage-ment's most important role is tracking, forecasting, and administration. Even sales represen-tatives typically perceive management's primary role not as coach and "mentor" but as "the sales police."

The problem is one of *measurement* and *perceptions*. Just how necessary and, more impor-tant, how *effective* is the sales manager in the selling process? What part of sales revenues can be directly attributed to the guidance of sales management? How much management time needs to be spent in coaching, motivating, and face-to-face time with customers to produce maximum results?

We asked a group of salespeople this question: "How effective is the coaching you receive from your manager in helping you close sales?" These were some of the answers:

- "Not very. Times have changed since he/she was out in the field!"
- "My manager is only concerned with what's going to close this month."
- "Coaching? I spend most of my time educating my manager."
- "I usually don't hear anything I haven't already thought of."
- "Coaching sessions just take time away from selling."
- "He/she doesn't know what's going on, and I don't have the time to tell him/her."

The truth lies in understanding just how difficult the job of sales management really is. As we've said, most managers are personally focused on helping drive sales and making salespeople more successful, and they want to do this through better coaching and mentoring. Despite all the good intentions, however, managers are still too often overwhelmed with administration and have far less knowledge than they need to be effective coaches about "what's really going on out there."

> The only way I know what's really going on in the sales territories is through the call reports I have the reps fill out, and of course by talking to them. Frankly that's not always a lot of information, often late—and reporting does take time away from their selling.

As sales automation comes to sales organizations, an important benefit will be the return of *real-time* sales progress information direct to managers, without requiring sales reporting other than that which the salespeople do for themselves.

This creates new paradigms for management:

1. Far fewer sales managers will in fact be needed to *track and monitor* sales activities.
2. Managers will have the information available that they need to be more effective coaches, without the necessity of cumbersome and time-consuming manual call reports, forecasts, and "how's it going?" sessions with the salespeople.
3. Ninety percent of the job of the new sales manager will truly be as a *coach*.

If that were all there was to it, then it would be easy. Managers armed with better information must spend more of their time coaching, in the field, and with customers. It's unfortunately not that simple. Traditional sales coaching and motivational techniques will prove to be painfully inadequate. "Here's an idea you might try" won't cut it anymore. The "high-value" manager will have become a *master strategist*, a sales resource armed with a broad base of information, experience, and outstanding strategic planning skills—a manager who is continuously monitoring trends, sales progress, and competitive activity. The analogy is not unlike a modern general who directs the course of battle using advanced C3I (command, control, communication, and intelligence) technology that provides real-time battlefield information.

The general-of-the-army analogy is helpful in another way as well. It's one thing to have information available, but it's entirely another thing to know how to use it most effectively. No general takes charge without a firm grounding in military strategies and tactics. The "new breed" of sales manager is going to need a "war college" education that few, if any, have received to date.

FIGURE 3.1. THE MANAGER'S ROLE

Managing is not "tracking."

Managing is providing a *recognized source of competitive advantage* to the salesperson.

In the new sales environment, the only purpose and justification of management is to provide clear and measurable added value to the salesperson, nothing more and nothing less.

The future is about creating a new sales representative–sales management partnership of strategies and tactics that delivers more sales revenues with higher margins in less time. The change begins by rethinking the way we measure sales performance.

MEASURING SALES PERFORMANCE: THREE MODELS

Since selling began, every company, every sales manager, and every salesperson has wrestled with the question of how best to measure, coach, and track sales performance. Sales automation technology enables three models for performance management—one may prove to be self-defeating and two others, in combination, have a real potential for long-term sales and even corporate benefit.

MODEL 1: ACTIVITY MANAGEMENT OR BUSINESS-AS-USUAL

Traditionally, sales managers have measured performance *by the numbers*, using visible indicators of sales progress:

1. Number of calls made per day, week, and month
2. Leads received and followed-up,
3. Demonstrations/presentations given
4. Proposals generated and delivered
5. Sales revenue dollar numbers achieved

As SFA systems make this information available almost as it is generated, an apparent *simple solution* to improving performance comes to mind: *manage more tightly, correct problems quicker (before they get out of hand), and keep people on track and on the "numbers."* Not surprisingly, in the infancy of sales automation systems, this capability was part of many software vendor's marketing message (*Control* your sales force!). It also explains why so many sales reps were turned off to the entire automation concept.

Some managers (as well as salespeople) believe in and live by the axiom, "the numbers will set you free." In short, if you make the right number of calls and do a sufficient number of other specific sales activities consistently day in and day out, sales will naturally follow.

MYTH: The "numbers" will set you free!
REALITY: The M.A.Z.E.

For example, a company calculates from its historical sales data and reports that for every 100 telephone sales contacts made by a salesperson the following results are achieved on the average:

100 telephone sales contacts *convert into*
25 initial sales calls that *convert into*
10 prospects that *convert into*
5 proposals delivered that *convert into*
1 sale closed with an average value of $10,000.

Calculating backward then, to make an annual sales quota of $500,000 would require an average of 50 closed sales initially generated by 5,000 telephone sales contacts, or approximately 20 phone calls each day.

Given these statistics, management sets a minimum daily activity requirement that each salesperson make twenty cold prospecting phone calls. It's a reasonable theory and has some level of validity; that is, making sales does require some critical activity level. But this kind of activity management ignores the *Sales Success = Quality x Execution* formula. More important, in terms of assuring and *maximizing* sales performance, we will see that it just doesn't hold up at all.

Also known as "Attila the Hun Rides Again" management, activity management using sales automation to achieve a new level of activity *micromanagement* can be absolutely guaranteed to produce the following results:

1. **Sales resistance to automation.** The tool is clearly for the benefit of management, not the salespeople.
2. **Massively inaccurate data.** One way or another, you can be sure that the activity data recorded by the salespeople *will show that the required number of daily calls were made,* which in the final analysis benefits no one, especially the sales manager.
3. **Demotivation of the sales force.** Management becomes the "sales police," not the coaching staff.

Here is the problem. Activity measurement and micromanagement are very easy with sales automation technology, and it's the way things have always been done, just faster and with less work! So, for the most part, it's perceived as the natural and logical model for most companies and managers to use as they automate and manage the sales force. But the bottom line is that it just won't work—and that has been proven time and time again in virtually every company that has tried it.

MODEL 2: SALES PROCESS MANAGEMENT

The first model of performance management measured raw sales calls made and projected results based upon those numbers. "Sales process management" is a more viable model that focuses on a different set of activity measurements: the *type* and *frequency* of sales calls and the *speed* of sales progress. It also happens to be a management methodology naturally supported by sales automation technology.

For instance, in the first model we used an example of a very simplistic sales cycle or process made up of "sales milestones," that is, critical events that must be achieved in every successful sale. The cycle began with prospecting and progressed to an initial sales call, prospect qualification, proposal delivery, and finally to the close. We'll use that same example again, except that in sales process management, we will track the *rate of successful progress* through that sales cycle (process) as our indicator of probable sales success.

We're specifically interested in factors such as:

- The **time** it takes each sales opportunity to move from milestone to milestone in the sales cycle (and developing new strategies and sales tactics to speed it up).
- **"Failure points"**—identification of the specific milestones or steps at which opportunities are most often lost or which there appears to be the greatest difficulty in achieving (and developing strategies and tactics to better address these). For example, if a specific number of sales opportunities seems to have been lost following "demonstration" or "proposal" mile-

stones, we may want to look closely at these failure points to understand exactly what happened, why it happened, and to develop new strategies to address them.

The process model, then, is first and foremost a *quality-based* model that differs from the activity model of performance management with a fundamental assumption:

> **The most effective way to increase sales revenue production is not necessarily to increase the volume of prospects in the sales pipeline but rather to increase the number of successful sales cycles a salesperson can complete during the quota year.**

A Coaching Model.

The process model is primarily a *coaching model*. Sales management continuously tracks and evaluates sales activity and progress with the primary intent of assisting salespeople in developing the most effective sales strategies and tactics to advance to the next milestone.

Using process management combined with sales automation technology, a sales manager bases coaching strategies upon two fundamental pieces of information:

1. The immediate objective, which is the specific next milestone that must be reached in the sales cycle.
2. More complete and comprehensive knowledge of the prospect company, identification of key contacts, and a history of sales calls and activities completed so far.

Simply put, managers spend little time asking "How's it going?" or "What did you do last week?" and devote more time to discussing sales strategies and options with their salespeople—all with the single purpose of speeding the sales process and increasing the potential number of successful sales cycles.

M.A.Z.E. Theory

FIGURE 3.2

Salespeople get caught in
the
M.A.Z.E.
Maximum Activity Zero Effect

Why process management now? Because *effective* process management is now technologically possible and competitive advantage demands it. Perhaps the best example is the theory of the sales **M.A.Z.E.: Maximum Activity with Zero Effect**. In other words, the M.A.Z.E. illustrates what happens when salespeople approach selling without a solid process or plan and instead generate lots of sales activity that don't really go anywhere. It applies to managing sales territories, key accounts, and working individual sales opportunities.

I first started selling for the IBM Corporation in New England during the early 1970s and learned to prospect by "smokestacking," which I consider the ultimate example of being "lost in the M.A.Z.E." If you're not familiar with the term, it's a literal one. Each day, I would drive the highways and back roads of my assigned territory looking for industrial smokestacks rising above the trees. A smokestack meant that there was a company somewhere nearby, and I would proceed to find it and find someone there to talk to me about computers.

If you think that was an inefficient way to find business, you're right, but consider that for the most part neither I nor most other salespeople had any idea of what companies were located in our territories except for the few major manufacturers. The information just wasn't readily available! I got a little smarter as time went on by using Chamber of Commerce lists and business directories, but "smokestacking" was still the generally accepted method of prospecting — and one that my managers encouraged.

I was truly "lost in the M.A.Z.E." I made lots and lots of calls on almost anyone who would talk to me. I believed in "the numbers" — that if I made enough calls, I knew (prayed? hoped?) I'd finally "get lucky" and find a real, live, closable prospect. With enough of those I'd make my quota and the 100% Club. As the months went by and year-end loomed closer,

I became progressively more hysterical and looked even harder for new smokestacks. In the M.A.Z.E., sales success was measured by miles and luck.

Working sales opportunities, particularly in large accounts, had a lot in common with "smokestacking." I particularly remember getting lost in the M.A.Z.E. in a high-potential opportunity I found at American Can Company located in Greenwich, Connecticut (they had a big smokestack).

My manager explained to me that to make a sale in a large account, I needed to "be there."

"I want you to spend three days each week at American Can," he told me. "Really get to know them!"

"Who should I be calling on?" I asked.

"The important thing is that you're there. Get to know everybody you can. But remember that if we're going to win this business, YOU HAVE TO BE THERE! I expect to see that you're there *at least* three days a week!"

I spent *a lot* of time at American Can. I had an "office" in a back corner of their cafeteria. I talked to everyone who would willingly talk to me. I made many presentations and sales calls to convince them that we were the right people to do business with. I made a lot of good friends there, too. I never closed any business, but I had a lot of friends. The problem was that they weren't sure exactly why I was there — or what I was supposed to be doing — any more than I was. To make it worse, they canceled the project.

FIGURE 3.3. THE SOLUTION

THE SOLUTION TO THE M.A.Z.E.

FIND THE FASTEST ROUTE TO THE CLOSE!

I knew how to make great sales calls, but I didn't know how to really manage a sales opportunity, that is, to work the "deal" *to find the shortest route to the close*. In effect I was lost in the M.A.Z.E. because I had no process of sales milestones and no plan to achieve them. So I wasted time, my most valuable resource, as I wandered down blind alleys and in endless backtracking. To make it worse, I had no management support to have done anything else.

> **The solution to the M.A.Z.E. is the shortest route to the close.**
> **The shortest route to the close is the right sales process.**

In today's marketplace, what company wants or can afford to have salespeople selling this way — "smokestacking" and wandering through sales opportunities?

MODEL 3: PROFITABLE CUSTOMER RELATIONSHIP MANAGEMENT

The real problem with activity management or even process management is that even when it results in the sales "success" of closed business, there is no guarantee that the business will be profitable for the company or the customer. In other words, *good* business provides a profit to the seller and a recognized value (profit) to the buyer. Just as important, it results in a business relationship that ultimately leverages additional long-term sales. As obvious as this may sound, worthwhile short- and long-term business is generated only when *this* is what we manage. So from this perspective:

> **The real measure of sales performance is**
> **Profit + Recognized Customer Value**

A good example of this concept comes surprisingly from the sales force automation marketplace itself. In this segment of the software industry, sales automation implementations frequently begin with a small pilot roll-out — usually 5% to 10% of the total potential number of salespeople. Sometimes, however, the pilots have gone no further; that is, sales automation is never fully implemented with the entire sales force. While this can happen for a variety of reasons, most often the customers did not *perceive* the value they expected after being sold.

Perceive, of course, is the key word here. The customers had a set of expectations which they did not recognize as having been met to their satisfaction. Sometimes the seller has exactly the opposite impression and believes the customer is unrealistic, won't listen, or just "doesn't understand."

Regardless of who is really at fault, both the seller and the customer lose. However, the seller loses in three ways:

1. The pilot was often not a profitable deal by itself. The sales effort expended would have only been justified by the larger deal.
2. The long-term opportunity and the ability to do business with this customer in the future is effectively lost.
3. There is the "cost" of time that could have been better spent on other sales opportunities.

What happened? There are any number of possibilities:

- Someone unfortunately believed in the faulty sales axiom, "Don't confuse the sell with the install!" The objective was to close the business (revenue) now and worry about the appropriateness of the "product solution" to the customer's needs later.
- The customer's needs and wants were never understood or the expectations were never clearly set (for both seller and customer).
- The salesperson did not receive the right direction. Management failed (or was unable) to do "quality control" during the sales process to assure "good business" was being conducted by continuously tracking sales progress and assessing opportunity viability. Assuring that salespeople are focused on business that's good for the company and the customer can be temporarily frustrating for the sales rep, but it benefits everyone in the long term.
- The headlong dash for revenues, measured only by the activities necessary to "get the deal," never took into account either the immediate or the long-term *profitability* of the sales effort. How much sales effort and what expenditure of sales resources were going to be necessary to close, install, and support the sale? How long until enough revenues would be received before the sale could be considered profitable? What was the risk?

To ensure the real quality of business, then, continuous "Go, No Go" assessments of profitability and customer satisfaction potential need to have been made jointly by the sales rep and the sales manager.

FIGURE 3.4. THE MANAGER'S ROLE

Selling is not just "closing."

Selling is building *profitable customer relationships.*

The fundamental goal of selling in today's market must become the creation of **profitable customer relationships**. As much as that may sound like a typical throwaway phrase, consider it closely.

Profitable would seem to be an obvious goal, except that most salespeople are measured and paid on revenues, not profits or "quality" of the sale, that is, the fit and overall customer satisfaction. *Relationships* means the potential for a continuing business relationship with a customer. Further, it can mean the strategic value of that customer to leverage additional sales in other divisions, subsidiaries, or affiliates or with other companies in the marketplace. But if *profitable customer relationships* are not foremost in the thinking of our salespeople, they can hardly be blamed. After all, it's not what most are paid to do.

So the question remains: what kind of performance do we really want to measure? Activity? Profits? Satisfaction? Potential? Some combination of all of them?

A new and more critical role of *sales activity* management then is as a tool to

1. Track and measure resources expended (sales time, expenses, etc.).
2. Assure profitable sales.
3. Assess, track, and ensure customer satisfaction and long-term business potential.
4. Assure that we are spending the right amount of time, in the right accounts, and on the right opportunities to create the right results.

But There's Always a Catch!

Sales automation systems, when used between managers and salespeople as *joint sales planning and monitoring tools*, clearly offer the *capacity* to measure performance in terms of building more profitable customer relationships. That potentially represents an almost incalculable benefit to any company. To accomplish it, however, will require more than motivating and coaching. It will require rather far-reaching changes in many corporations:

1. Development of clear *sales profitability models* — how much resource can be expended per potential sales dollar revenue.

2. Restructuring the goals of salespeople to include *profit dollar quotas*, and managing the cultural change that will now define sales success as how quickly and effectively a salesperson can move through the maze of the sales cycle.

3. Restructuring the goals and payment of both sales and service representatives based upon customer retention and growth, recognizing that repeat business is invariably the most profitable and that a competitive loss is a corporate disaster.

4. Retraining managers as *investment managers* whose critical tasks are to allocate and monitor resources and to coach and mentor salespeople — and to be accountable for return-on-investment.

5. Making automation technology a permanent and required part of the corporate culture because ultimately it represents the *only way the necessary accurate profit and customer models can be maintained.*

WHY IS THIS SO CRITICAL?

Why is this kind of performance management so critical today? A few years ago, at the height of the economic recession of the late 1980s, I sat in on a board meeting of a large technical services corporation that was preparing to close its doors. The discussion centered around what had gone wrong. One manager put it this way, "We got too deeply involved in too many unprofitable deals. All we focused on was closing business; we didn't develop the solid customer relationships that could have pulled us through the hard times. Our customers see us as a *cost* that they can cut back, not as an important part of making them successful. And it's too late now to do anything about it."

THE STATE OF THE ART

Who is doing profitable customer relationship management today, and what are the results? In one sense, the effort is still in its infancy; new profitability management and monitoring models are under development paralleling the large-scale implementations of the sales automation technology needed to support them.

There are, however, some promising early results and leaders. A large, midwestern service provider was able to identify the 20% of the account base that was producing 80% of the *profits*. Direct salespeople now call only upon those accounts, while the remainder are serviced through other, less expensive sales channels. Future evaluations of how accounts will be serviced, directly or indirectly, will continue to be made through profitability assessment. And this is only the start.

FINAL THOUGHTS — THE BOTTOM LINE

Measuring performance today is basically easier than ever with sales automation technology. The issue is not "measuring performance" per se, but rather determining *what kind of performance you really want to measure*, and a willingness to face up to the necessary re-engineering effort and cultural change to achieve it.

As all these changes come into play, how will they affect the way we sell and manage day-to-day? How will we direct our salespeople? Both the process and the profitable customer relationship performance management models will be well served by BEST/NEXT™ — a powerful, new sales planning and coaching model.

CHAPTER 4

BEST/NEXT™ SELLING AND MENTOR MANAGEMENT

In day-to-day terms, most sales managers end up managing the past when what they really want to do is to *manage the future*. For example, when I've spoken at sales management conferences, I always ask the managers in the audience this question: "When you get back to the office, what is the first thing you're going to do?"

Of course, the answer always is either "Call the sales reps and find out what's happened while I was gone" or "See what's closed!"

As we have shown, sales automation technology, well used, is going to significantly reduce the manager's need to track down the sales reps to find out what's going on, or to rely on call reports that are often incomplete and out of date by the time they are received. So, armed with up-to-date sales *progress* data, the manager now has more time available and capability to manage the future, to coach and help the salespeople plan the most effective strategies and tactics. To do this, however, we need effective coaching techniques that can be supported by sales automation technology to help managers become "mentor" managers.

THE BEST/NEXT SALES PLANNING AND COACHING

FIGURE 4.1. THE CRUCIAL QUESTION

To answer this question:

"What is the Best thing to do Next?"
(to advance the sale)

Reduce the business of selling to its most basic concept. Throughout the sales process, the salesperson is continuously trying to find the best answer to one single question: What is the *best* possible thing that I can do *next* that will most effectively advance the sale closer to the close?

Read the question again. It is the essence of sales success.

When we have a set of defined sales process milestones in place, the BEST/NEXT task is to determine the sales tactics or actions that will most quickly advance us to the next milestone. If we could *always* determine and execute the BEST/NEXT sales tactics, we would win every deal or walk away before investing resources in the wrong opportunities.

BEST/NEXT is perhaps the simplest, yet most effective, coaching technique ever developed. Think of it this way:

> **The job of the salesperson is to develop and flawlessly execute the BEST/NEXT; the job of the sales manager is to assure that the sales rep's action plan is, in fact, the best possible course of action — and to support its execution with necessary resources.**

One of my clients has been extremely successful with utilizing BEST/NEXT as a sales planning tool for the salespeople and as a coaching system for the sales managers. They first added a special type of "To-Do" to their sales automation database, appropriately titled, "Best Next Plan." Doing so enabled the sales rep to record a detailed description of the current strategy and planned tactics.

Second, management instituted a firm policy:

> **For every active sales opportunity, there must be a current BEST/NEXT "To-Do" in place.**

In other words, as soon as one BEST/NEXT activity is completed, the salesperson is expected to *immediately* plan the next.

Third, weekly management coaching sessions became a *joint planning dialogue* between the salesperson and the manager based on assuring that the salesperson's plan was in fact the very best possible BEST/NEXT.

A typical coaching scenario — face-to-face or on the telephone — usually begins with the sales manager confirming to the salesperson that the manager has reviewed the key opportunities that the rep is currently working. Ideally, sales automation has provided the manager with up-to-date information on opportunity progress, recent sales activities performed by the salesperson, and the sales process milestone reached. The sales manager is able to ask any clarification questions he or she may have.

In the larger sense, this is *fact-based management* combined with *BEST/NEXT strategic thinking*. Through the capabilities of sales automation, sales managers make BEST/NEXT recommendations based on the wealth of "facts" of sales activity and progress provided by automation technology, not based on gut feelings.

A FACT-BASED BEST/NEXT COACHING SESSION

Anne S., a sales representative for ABC Co., and her manager "meet" every Tuesday afternoon from 1:30 P.M. to 2:00 P.M. to review Anne's accounts and current sales opportunities. Anne works from her home office in St. Louis, phoning in to her manager in New Hampshire. Both Anne and her manager share the sales automation database on their laptops and have her accounts displayed on the screen. They have both prepared for today's session by reviewing the top five accounts that Anne has forecast to close this month.

Before ABC Co. introduced sales automation, however, this was the typical conversation:

MANAGER: Bring me up to date, Anne, on each of the deals you plan to close this month.

ANNE: Okay. Well, first there's XYZ Co., and I feel good about this one. Remember how last week I was trying to get in to see the purchasing agent? Well ... .

Anne begins the tedious process of educating her manager on the progress she has made.

MANAGER: Why did you do that? Did you think about ... ? What are you going to do next?

Much of their half hour was spent bringing the manager up-to-date on what has happened during the last week, focusing on the past. Not only were her manager's "coaching" suggestions spur of the moment, Anne, like most salespeople, approached these sessions with a "Gotcha!" mentality—her manager was reviewing her performance looking for a "Gotcha!" to correct what she could have done better.

Today, with automation and BEST/NEXT opportunity management, the conversation and the results have changed.

MANAGER: Okay, Anne, let's look first at the account you have as the highest probability of closing for this month, XYZ Co. I can see here that your plan to get in and see the purchasing agent was successful and it says here that he sees no problems with cutting a P.O. by next week. Anything more you want to add?

ANNE: It was a good call. As I indicated, he does not meet with most vendors personally, so I felt this was a good sign.

MANAGER: Based on that, Anne, I tend to agree with you that this deal is an "A" account on the forecast. I've reviewed your BEST/NEXT strategy that you plan to meet this week with XYZ's president to wrap the deal, and I think you have some good ideas. Let me give you some suggestions on how you may want to approach him.

This was a true fact-based *coaching* session. The intent was to find ways to move the sale ahead, and focus on *facts*, not on making management feel good about the progress of this sale. Anne and her manager have moved away from "Gotcha!" to "mentor" management.

This session worked for both Anne and her manager because the customer sales progress information was accurate and up-to-date, allowing her manager to review the data before their meeting and formulate specific questions and ideas to help her advance the sale.

But what if Anne didn't want to use the system? What if she was busy and didn't have a chance to update the record fully (or at all) before the coaching session? That simply wouldn't have happened because Anne's manager relies on sales automation.

MANAGER: Okay, Anne, let's look first at the account you have as the highest probability of closing for this month, XYZ Co. I can see here that you were not able to get in and see the purchasing agent. That's too bad. Maybe you should … .

ANNE: No, I did get in, and it was great. I just was a little busy, and I didn't get around to putting it in the computer. Let me tell you all about it! I … .

MANAGER: Excuse me, Anne. You're wasting our time. The purpose of our meeting is to plan together what to do next to close this deal, not to tell me what you've been doing. Besides that, Anne, I spent considerable time trying to develop some ideas to help you get in to see that purchasing agent, and apparently that was another waste of my time.

The coaching process, then, is one of joint *negotiation*. The sales rep and the sales manager work together to assure that the most effective strategy is in place.

The BEST/NEXT methodology results in five important benefits:

1. It *forces* salespeople to at least *begin thinking strategically*, to think out and plan their actions and be willing to discuss and justify their decisions.
2. It clearly changes the management role from the "sales police" to a *competitive resource*.
3. It redefines the interaction between salesperson and manager — and potentially within an entire sales unit — toward planning and working as a team.
4. Sales automation assures that the sales manager is no longer considered "out of touch" with what is happening in the field.
5. It creates an *audit trail* of sales plans and related activities to accomplish them. This provides

both sales reps and managers a powerful win/loss analysis tool for debriefing not only lost sales but also "wins" to better understand what was done that made the competitive difference. This is especially so when the history, or BEST/NEXT strategies, and completed activities are accessible in a sales automation database.

There is another benefit of BEST/NEXT coaching for sales managers that becomes readily apparent after the technique has been used for even a short time — *sales rep assessment*.

Sales managers who use the BEST/NEXT approach consistently will learn that they have three kinds of salespeople working for them.

Type 1: A Manager's Dream.

Most managers find as they use BEST/NEXT that, on the average, about 20% of their salespeople *really know what they are doing*! As we review their plans and strategies, it is clear that they are well thought out and, with only minimal management guidance, really are the *best* possible courses of action. In large part the management response to these kinds of reps is "Go forth my children and sell, and call me if you need anything at all!"

Type 2: The Reps Who Need You.

Usually a majority of the sales reps — about 60% — can use some management advice and direction. They are fully capable of developing solid BEST/NEXT tactics, but they can benefit from a sales manager's experience and knowledge of what other salespeople are doing that is and isn't working in past and other current sales opportunities.

Initially these salespeople may require a fair amount of support if only because many are unused to planning formally. It is important for a manager to ask the questions, "Why do you think that this is the best course of action?" and "How will this action help you advance more rapidly to the close?" on a regular basis during coaching sessions. The purpose is not only to assure the BEST/NEXT but also to help them develop this kind of strategic thinking.

There is a potential motivator from this planning and coaching method as well, which is particularly useful in large accounts or sales that have very long sell cycles. I often personally experienced motivation down times in my own experience in complex sales to large accounts, in part because success was measured by as little as one or two closed sales each year. Often by the time the sale was completed, I felt more relief than elation. In other words, it can be hard to stay motivated when "closes" are so far apart.

FIGURE 4.2. THE BEST/NEXT STEPS

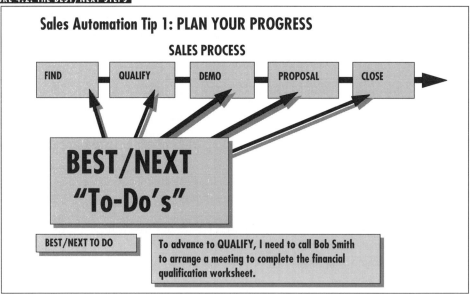

Using BEST/NEXT planning combined with established sales process milestones creates a *series of mini-goals* that are not reached by luck or hard work but rather by successful planning and excellent execution by the salesperson. This can provide salespeople with a series of short-term "wins" that provide a feeling of success and a sense that the opportunity is visibly *progressing*—a perception that is not always clear in long-term opportunities.

Type 3: A Manager's Nightmare.

Unfortunately there will be some salespeople who, as their manager reviews their BEST/NEXT strategies, *clearly have no idea what they are doing*! In other words, their approach to territory and account development is making lots and lots of sales calls in the hope that enough will pay off to make quota. They are lost deep in the M.A.Z.E.!

This may indicate sales reps who are clearly incompetent, and their managers will have to make some decisions if they are prepared to expend the resources to develop these reps. Surprisingly, however, these are not always unsuccessful salespeople. In fact, they may have outstanding personal sales skills and have established a long track record of success selling in just this way. What is *not* surprising is that these are the very people who most resist management tracking and coaching because fundamentally they have no real plan for success.

What is important to remember is that in today's changing market, it is getting harder and harder to be successful in sales by effectively "smokestacking" through the territory and sales opportunities. Sales reps who refuse to look at themselves as a business will rapidly lose competitive advantage to those who will.

USING BEST/NEXT — ONE FOR ALL

BEST/NEXT is not a coaching tool just for use with reps who are not selling well. This concept of planning is a way of doing business — and it only really works when it becomes an integral part of the corporate culture. It becomes a way of thinking and even a way of talking throughout the sales organization. Most important, it gets real results through generating a higher percentage of closed sales achieved in less time. Additionally, management support for BEST/NEXT coaching also can play a significant role in assuring that salespeople actively and consistently utilize sales automation.

MENTOR MANAGEMENT

There are some important final points and techniques worth bringing out from the combination of BEST/NEXT coaching and sales automation technology, and what that really means to the changing job of sales management, which may be redefined as **mentor management**:

- **Accountability.** BEST/NEXT and SFA create a new accountability between the salesperson and the manager. Forecasts and action plans are based upon a wealth of facts as recorded by the salesperson, but the accuracy and value of forecasts and plans are only as good as the quality of the information in the system and the strategic thinking applied to it. A manager, too, has a new accountability to the salesperson to be well informed and to provide well thought-out guidance, as well as greater accountability to corporate for greater forecast accuracy, more specific identification of opportunities and issues, and so forth.

- **Management Preparation and Analytical Skills.** Fact-based management enhances the role of sales managers as strategists and tacticians and lessens their role as "activity managers." Managers must spend the majority of time reviewing the status and development of sales opportunities, identifying successful and unsuccessful tactics, and conducting coaching sessions.

- **Mentor Management and Coaching.** In the selling process, managers will need to assume a new role as a "Mentor" instead of a "Gotcha!" manager. This will mean creating a new, often initially foreign, relationship with salespeople. The manager and the salesperson must become a "strategic team," together applying their common skills and knowledge to advance and close the sale. By itself this will be one of the most difficult tasks for sales management — and necessary to eliminate the "Big Brother" mentality.

How do salespeople react to a fact-based management style? Greater accountability and management involvement may initially be viewed as taking away a sales rep's traditional independence. However, salespeople who are managed this way find they not only close more business (because they are receiving increased help and resources) but also they are actually *empowered* (and in some ways have increased independence) through less reporting and less time spent keeping their managers up-to-date. Salespeople who know what they are doing and are doing it well will likely receive less management attention than they do today simply because they don't need it. It turns out that "Big Brother"—especially for good salespeople—is far more myth than reality.

CREATING MENTOR MANAGEMENT AND SALES ACCEPTANCE

Becoming a mentor manager isn't always easy. It is not only a change in technique but also a change in the culture of the sales team. Here are some basic principles for mentor manager "wanna-be's":

- **Don't confuse "mentor" with "buddy."** By definition, the role of a manager is somewhat authoritarian, responsible for returning goaled revenues to the corporation. For a mentor manager, the best way to achieve this goal is to use his or her experience and skills to make salespeople more successful. This means becoming a "best resource," not a "best friend."

- **Glue your computer to your hip.** Well, not literally, but as far as SFA goes, salespeople will use it *as well and as often as they perceive it is used by management.* In short, it's not enough for a manager to use SFA for tracking, analysis, and planning behind closed doors (in the office or at home). The manager's laptop computer must become the "bible" of sales activity. It travels visibly with the manager at all times. Whenever an account is discussed, the manager refers to the system. During coaching sessions (especially face-to-face), the system is the primary discussion tool for developing and clarifying BEST/NEXT strategies and tactics.

- **Visibly increase your personal "Q" factor.** As in the success equation, Q is for "Quality." In a survey of salespeople regarding their opinion of their direct manager's quality, many responded that they felt managers were out of touch, didn't really know what was going on in the field, returned little value to the salesperson from the information and reports sent in, and that "times have changed since he or she was selling." In short, it's not enough for managers simply to have better information at hand; they have to visibly and effectively use that information.

- **Develop plans for success supported by facts.** Salespeople *want* to feel that management has a plan for success; nevertheless, many are skeptical of the "sales strategy of the week" that comes from "Corporate Disconnect"—namely, "Management doesn't really know what it's doing." Mentor managers are more successful and find greater sales acceptance with the plans they develop simply because they are known to be based on comprehensive field data provided by the salespeople themselves.

- **Compliment and counsel.** This is a simple technique that is an essential tool of mentor managers. In the process of opportunity review and BEST/NEXT coaching, it's all too easy to quickly find fault ("You should have done this or that!") and create an instantaneous "Big Brother" reaction. In the coaching process, find two or three things to compliment a person on before counseling him or her on what might have been done better. For example, "Bob, this looks like an excellent new opportunity you've developed, and you've certainly qualified it well. What I am concerned about is … ."

- **Conduct "The Sales Team Strategy Session."** This fundamental technique for managers and salespeople eases the process of change. It's critical that salespeople feel they are a part of the process when new methodologies and technologies are introduced to the organization. The problem arises when we bring them in at the assessment and planning phase ("Tell us what we should do and whether you like it"). This doesn't mean that we should not ask for input when evaluating potential new methodologies or technologies, but many companies involve the reps at this point to head off resistance (which it doesn't—it just gives them time to figure out strategies to beat it!).

Once a decision has been made, that is the time to involve the salespeople in order to elicit their help in making it work! In other words, "We in management have decided on a program which will be part of how we sell. The joint task before all of us is to make this program successful. Together we want to develop a strategy to make this happen!" Notice that this is distinctly different from "Let's sell the reps on the new program!" This technique is "The Four-Step Process." The example provided is geared to implementing sales automation, but it is equally applicable to any sales or corporate program. It is a critical skill for "mentor managers."

THE FOUR-STEP PROCESS

STEP 1: THE TOP MANAGEMENT MANDATE

Critical to the long-term success of an SFA project (or implementation of a new selling/managing methodology) is to quickly establish an initial base of 100% sales management and sales rep users. This is true whether automation is being rolled out to a pilot group or to an entire sales force. In addition, we want to make it clear throughout the organization that the new systems and processes are not optional! They are not on trial or are being tested (although they will continue to be refined and improved). They will be a permanent part of the corporate culture. There are large-scale corporate reasons that make this project essential to the company.

This message *absolutely* must come from top corporate management, not only because of its weight but also because a top management mandate empowers sales managers to require full SFA use by making it a part of their goals as well.

Certainly this kind of mandate will not produce the level of *quality* users needed—and at this point, that's okay—but it does create the starting point for developing a more complete corporate sales database from which the sales automation system can be further tuned and refined.

STEP 2: THE SALES TEAM STRATEGY SESSION

At the same time as we are mandating automation and other processes, we would like to begin developing a strong sense of ownership by the sales force, especially because we want our tuning and refining efforts to reflect the needs and wants of sales as much as possible. The Sales Team Strategy Session begins this process and requires a visible commitment by salespeople to make the new systems successful.

The Sales Team Strategy Session may be conducted at any time, but it is perhaps most effective in conjunction with initial roll-out or user training. Led by the first-line sales manager, the session is attended by direct report salespeople and other cross-functional personnel who may have an interest or eventual role in the project, with the exception of senior management who should not attend at this point.

The steps of elements of the session are as follows:

1. **Company Values: Setting the Stage.** Begin with a restatement by the manager of the corporate mandate and the reasons why the project is critical to the success of the entire company. "SFA is not an option. Our purpose today is, as a team, to determine how to make this new system work for *us*! The company is committed to the success of this project, and I have personally committed us to its success!"

2. **Identify the Sales Unit's Challenges in the Marketplace.** The manager conducts a group discussion to identify the major challenges this *specific* sales team faces in its marketplace, such as competition, leads, demographics, or customer satisfaction. All of these are issues which are affecting each sales rep's success and which need to be resolved!

3. **Identify High-Value Automation Solutions.** The manager and reps identify and apply the characteristics and functions of the SFA system (or process) which will be valuable in providing solutions to the *identified unit challenges*.

4. **Identify the Sales Manager's Needs and Challenges.** The sales manager is part of the sales team as well. Salespeople need to understand the issues that face their manager as part of the team-building concept that success is a group goal! For example, the manager may discuss the need to improve forecast accuracy, what it takes to obtain resources needed by the sales unit, or the corporate requirement for strategic planning. Identify SFA characteristics that address these as well. "As a team (manager and salespeople) we have both unique and common goals to address working together and toward which sales automation can be of value."

5. **Establish Team Rules and Tasks.** As a team, establish and agree upon the functional rules and tasks to make the new system or process successful in the unit, such as everyone will use SFA, weekly coaching session times and data requirements established, incentives and/or consequences defined.

6. **Statement of Position.** This is the most important element of the team strategy session. The

sales unit creates a unit Statement of Position which summarizes each of the above elements and details how the team has committed to make SFA successful. The team makes a formal presentation to senior management or creates a document for submission.

The fundamental results of the Sales Team Strategy Session are that management expectations are set and clearly apply to *everyone*, team interdependencies are defined and formed, management's requirements are more clearly understood, team members have had a role in determining how best to utilize new processes and systems, and most important, the team has delivered a public commitment to success. At this point, we have provided the sales manager a foundation on which to work.

The Sales Team Strategy Session can be even more effective when multiple sales units conduct their sessions simultaneously, for example, at a regional or national sales meeting. As each sales unit makes its final presentation to senior management before the entire group, all sales teams are exposed to a variety of creative strategies and ideas.

STEP 3: THE MANAGER-DEPENDENT SYSTEM

Initial success of any new program is dependent upon "enforcement" by the sales manager! The good news is that, if done right, it isn't a permanent condition and will become a self-reinforcing part of the "corporate culture"—again, *if it's done right!*

Once a 100% user base has been initially established and the team strategy session completed, the job of building quality begins, specifically improving the quantity and quality of data being entered and the processes used by the sales representatives. This task falls to the first-line sales managers and will be the direct result of managers' utilizing *fact-based management* techniques.

> **The level of quality and completeness that the manager requires in order to better do his or her job of managing will directly determine the quality level of the users.**

Users who have been moderates or skeptics begin to perceive the value of the new processes and systems when they see it used (and are required to use it) at a high-quality level of data.

The message to managers is clear: Lead by example!

STEP 4: THE PEER-MANAGED SYSTEM

As we discussed earlier, one of management's automation tasks will be to develop a team environment and mutual sharing of critical sales information (large-account team selling, competitive intelligence, lead distribution, industry data, and so forth). In some cases, teams may also include service and customer support field personnel who need to share and exchange account information with sales. As the team environment is built over time, inter-dependencies among team members are created. Like the sales manager, members count on the completeness and accuracy of SFA information in order to do their jobs. In short, the use and quality of SFA is mandated and managed by peers, not only by management.

Peer-managed systems are not built overnight and are the result of long-term corporate and sales management commitment. They are, however, virtually self-perpetuating, once they have become a permanent part of the corporate culture, and they represent a critical goal of sales force automation.

CHAPTER 5

ADDED-VALUE SELLING

THE BEST/NEXT QUESTION AND THE VALUE ANSWER

The question many potential mentor managers ask is, "What *is* the BEST/NEXT?" How do managers know? Relying on real-life experience will always be the manager's and sales rep's most important tool. Above and beyond that, however, the answer to the BEST/NEXT question will always be:

> **The BEST/NEXT tactic is always the one that enhances the customers' perception of the *unique value* we provide them!**

But what is **value**? Value is the source of competitive advantage!

So competitive advantage is simply what business and selling are all about. Lacking it creates a state of *competitive disadvantage* (do something quickly or get out of business) or *competitive parity* (the business "elephant graveyard"). Ultimately, advantage can only come from three possible sources. The first two are the most temporary and actually the weakest—the products we sell and the services we offer. The third, the strongest and most permanent, is the advantage created by our people in the form of the perceptions of our worth or value in the eyes of our prospects and customers.

In business today there is no competitive advantage program more prevalent—and no term more used—than *added-value*. In the course of scores of talks I've given in the last few years to various industry groups, I always ask the question, "How many of you have added-value programs actively in place?" Every hand goes up. When I ask, "How many of you think added-value is your key to competitive advantage?" every hand goes up. Then I ask, "Who can really define *value* (forget the 'added' part) and how to recognize it when you see it?" Most of the hands stay down. Hmm.

If the primary task of sales management is coaching, the question is "Exactly what is the subject of our coaching?" Sales call skills? Prospecting? Territory management? Account planning? Sales strategies? The answer, of course, is all of these, but to synthesize it, *coaching is the task of assuring that sufficient value is presented to and perceived by the customer to establish maximum competitive advantage and leverage the buying decision.*

PROVIDING VALUE

Among the most used (and vaguest) words in modern business vocabulary that describe competitive advantage are *quality* and *value*. They're nice words, suitable for almost any business occasion. Who can disagree with a great marketing statement such as, "We're working to improve overall *quality* so that we can offer our customers real *added value*"? You may not really understand it or believe it, but you can't argue with it.

Ask someone to define *quality* or *value*, and the answer is often not a great deal clearer: "Quality is doing things better, more efficiently and productively; value is giving the customers what they need." That's nice. We should all be more "efficient" (whatever that means!), and everyone should get what he or she needs (whatever *that* is!).

It's not surprising, then, that customers often regard the quality and added-value programs of their suppliers as so much smoke and mirrors. One customer even described vendors' added-value programs as "too many solutions in search of nonexistent problems!" Even salespeople may regard these programs as marketing copy instead of something they can get their hands around to drive more business. They are simply too nebulous.

Providing the customer with value—and assuring the customer's perception and recognition of it—is today the quintessential measure of competitive advantage. It can be argued that value is the true and primary product of any salesperson and that the physical products or services offered for sale are, in a sense, almost secondary to making the sale. But to accomplish this, *added-value* needs to be far more specifically defined. Not even the world's greatest salespeople can sell something they cannot clearly define to the customer or to themselves.

FIGURE 5.1. VALUE: THE COMPETITIVE ADVANTAGE

VALUE VS. LOVE

Many companies and their sales reps confuse *value* with *love*. They believe they provide added-value because their customers *like* them: The customer *likes* the salesperson who has developed a strong personal relationship with them; they feel that everyone at the company is responsive to them and wants to keep them happy; they've been able to negotiate a fair and honest deal; they believe that the vendor truly *values* their business. In short, there seems to be a virtual lovefest going on here. With all this liking and valuing going on, how can it be, then, that these customers could go to the competition? Why would they even listen to a competitor's "pitch"? But they actually sometimes do!

"Don't they appreciate all the value we gave them?"

"Where did we fail? We didn't know they were unhappy!"

"Didn't we make a strong enough effort to keep that customer?"

"Didn't we love them enough? We were there all the time!"

"What more do they want from us?"

"As Mary walked out the door, her suitcase in her hand, John cried out to her, 'Mary, how can you leave me? I thought you loved me!' Mary replied, 'I do love you, John, but I just can't live with you. I have other needs.'"

One of the most famous and most cited quotes of selling philosophy came from Thomas J. Watson of the IBM Corporation. Watson's philosophy was simple and, for better or worse, has guided generations of salespeople: "People buy from people they like!"

FIGURE 5.2. WATSON'S LAW

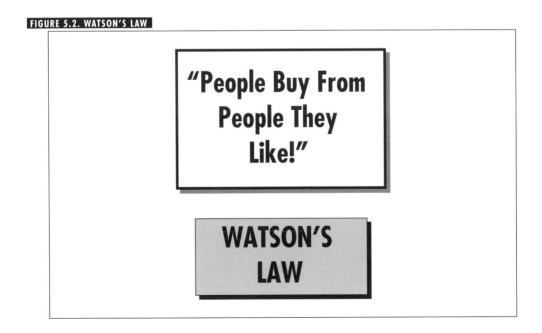

63

It's true, of course. People do buy from people they like. Unfortunately, they also sometimes quit buying from people they like and buy instead from people they don't like nearly as much. Believe it or not, they sometimes even buy from people they don't particularly like at all. In short, being liked is nice, but it's not enough.

> **McMahon's Corollary:**
> **"People buy from people they don't completely despise."**

Being liked by a customer is without a doubt a real sales advantage and is without question more advantageous than being hated. Attaining the status of best-liked salesperson or vendor, however, is not a guarantee of either winning the business or being able to keep it.

VALUE IS "NEED"

There is often a real difference between what people *like* and what they believe they really *need*. Moreover, when all is said and done, most business people differentiate quite clearly between what they like or want personally and the needs of their business, and they ultimately choose business!

FIGURE 5.3. MCMAHON'S REVISED LAW

" People Buy from
People They
NEED! "

**MCMAHON'S
REVISION**

When key decisions are made, the perceived needs of the business come first. In other words, as important as the value is that the vendor or supplier feels he or she provides the customer, how *critical to the needs of the business* does the customer perceive the products, services, and added-value? Are they "nice-to-have" or "got-to-have"?

THE VALUE/NEED TEST

What are your customer's perceptions of you, your company, and your products? You may feel you're doing a good job and have a good relationship with your customer, but are you "competition-proof"? To find out honestly, ask yourself these questions:

1. Would my customers say that they consider me, my company, and my product *essential* to the success of their business?

2. Would my customers say that separating from doing business with us could potentially do harm to their business?

3. Could my customers define what we offer — other than price or product features — that makes us valuable to their business operations?

4. If competitors call on my customers claiming a better product, a lower price, or a special offer, will my customers seriously look at them?

Are these unrealistic questions? Some might say so. Favorable answers would represent the perfect (and probably unachievable) customer relationship. This is certainly true if what we're selling is "product" instead of "value." Salespeople who understand and sell value, however—no matter what physical product or service they sell—can, in fact, confidently expect loyal and favorable answers to most or all of the questions.

I have had clients who actually told me when the competition stopped by and what "a great deal" they offered. They also told me, however, that there was "no way" they would have considered buying from them. You might think they did this to gain some leverage, but not so! Usually they reminded me why it was that they were my customers—because of the unique value they believed I provided (not just a few product features or cheaper price). Then they would pass along some competitive information they thought I could use.

Amazing! My customers want me to be successful because they believe that's what I want for them! They also recognize that my success is important to theirs. That's "competition-proofing."

Competition-proofing through customer-perceived value has obvious benefits: more sales to the account, less lost business that has to be made up somewhere else, and a reference source. But there is another, even more tangible benefit—time—the salesperson's most valuable resource.

Even satisfied customers are vulnerable to competitive intrusion when they do not feel that we are critical to their business success. In short, they're always willing to listen to a good marketing pitch. Given that, as salespeople, we have to spend a significant amount of sales time "checking up" on our customers to head off competitive intrusion before it can take hold. A competition-proofed customer base simply makes more time available for selling, and that translates into greater sales revenues.

Generations of salespeople have been taught that selling is a *personal* skill; that is, we make a sale by focusing on the needs and "pain" of the individual and applying solid interpersonal sales skills. This is still true, but today's customers look for stronger business reasons to back up their personal preferences. Providing recognized *critical business value* not only makes the initial sale, but also it keeps the customer.

> **The measure of value provided is how well the customer believes that the value fulfills the critical needs of the business and positively affects their success.**

THE RULES OF ADDED-VALUE SELLING

"We'll improve our competitive position and sell more if we offer more added-value to our customers. So let's give them more."

Giving customers more of anything—more service, more personal calls, special "help" lines, and the like—won't necessarily create value. Unfortunately, giving them more for their money is a pretty common approach to the added-value challenge. Unless the customers clearly *perceive* that "more" has a positive impact in helping them deal with their critical business issues (it makes them more successful), the only effect of providing more is lowering the seller's profit margins. Therefore, it is essential to understand the absolute rules of added-value selling.

> **FIRST ABSOLUTE RULE OF ADDED-VALUE SELLING:**
> **If your sales strategy is added-value, you *cannot* discount price!**

One large company almost put itself out of business by failing to understand and follow the first absolute rule. The sales force very effectively delivered the company's added-value suite of services (essentially more for less and lots of attention and service) to their customers. This, of course, increased the cost of sales. The company, however, felt confident that it represented a worthwhile investment; it would help generate additional business and reduce competitive losses. At the same time, however, salespeople and their managers continued to discount when faced with competitive pricing. The result? Costs increased; margin decreased; profits tumbled. The message? *You can do one or the other, but you can't do both!*

A decision has to be made. If you are a commodity and sell on product and price alone, you may be able to discount. If you are an added-value company, discounting is not an option!

> **SECOND ABSOLUTE RULE OF ADDED-VALUE SELLING:**
> **The objective of added-value selling is to justify the highest possible price!**

I recently conducted a sales strategy session for a client in which we focused on developing tactics to close several current key opportunities. They have a well thought-out added-value program that appears to be well received by their customer base. I asked one sales rep to describe the biggest issue he faced with a current sales opportunity and what his strategy was to address it.

"The problem," he said, "is that the competition's price is 5% lower than ours."

"And your solution is … ?" I asked.

"Well, I think if we can get within 2%, I can close it!"

Everyone in the room nodded. It seemed a reasonable approach, but was it? Imagine the faces when I responded that the strategy was totally unacceptable!

"Your objective," I said, "is to win the business and realize as much revenue for your company and yourself as possible. Your goal shouldn't be to see how close to the competition's price you can get. What you want to do is figure out how you can be not 5% more expensive but 10% or 15% more expensive — and absolutely justify it to the customer! That is how both you and your company prosper — higher commissions and higher profits."

Anyone can lower price. It's always been the easy out. Selling product and added-value at a fair price that reflects its benefit to the customer is what selling is really all about.

THIRD ABSOLUTE RULE OF ADDED-VALUE SELLING:
Profit is the name of the game!

Profitable customer relationships. Without profits there will shortly be no company; if there is no company, there is no job for the salesperson. Customers actually do understand and respect the necessity of profits, both yours and theirs. Few really expect something for nothing, although they'll take it if it's offered or believe they can get it. More important, if they truly value the vendor as important to the success of their business, they *want* you to make a fair profit.

FOURTH ABSOLUTE RULE OF ADDED-VALUE SELLING:
If you still feel the urge to discount price,
you don't believe in the value you provide!

I overheard a conversation between a sales rep and one of his company's application consultants. The consultant, a salaried employee, provided post-sale consulting services and customer training. The company normally charged a consulting fee of $1,500.00/day for her services.

The salesperson was attempting to get the application consultant to agree to do three days of training at no charge as an incentive to get a prospect to close. The consultant stubbornly refused to see why she should give away her services.

What hit me as I listened was that the consultant believed in the real value of what she offered, and she saw no good reason for giving it away. The salesperson, however, who should have been looking at the consultant's services as a way to increase his commissions, was effectively trying to lower the price—and lower commission and profit margin—in order to get the business. In short, the wrong person believed in the value of what the company was selling!

Before we can ask a customer to buy from us and perceive the benefits of our unique added-value, we have to believe in that value ourselves with the power and absolute conviction of an evangelist. In other words, there's got to be a lot more there than marketing copy!

So, putting it all together:

- Being liked does not create real competitive advantage, and love is not the same as value.
- Focus salespeople on developing competitive advantage through added-value efforts that customers perceive they really need.
- Base your coaching on providing necessary value to prospects and customers through salespeople's sales activities. Avoid managing based on activities that have no clear strategic purpose.
- Ask the BEST/NEXT question: "If you do (sales activity), how will the customer perceive the unique value provided?"

THE NINE CRITICAL BUSINESS NEEDS

So far we have somewhat begged the question of exactly what value is. In fact, what does constitute value in the mind of the customer? It's well and good to say that we must sell it; it is another thing entirely to define it specifically. If value, like beauty, is in the eye of the beholder, then…

Value is our product!

On the other hand, if value is defined as our ability to help a customer's business succeed, then we can begin to quantify and qualify it in terms of *critical business needs* that we can sell as *value products* to our prospects.

Every business in any industry—retailer, wholesaler, manufacturer, or service provider—has nine fundamental and critical needs. Successfully addressing each one of these is an absolute requirement for business success; failure to do so will ultimately bring business failure. It's as simple as that.

A vendor's or supplier's *value*—and competitive position—is really the result of how the seller can help the customer address these needs and how significant the customer *perceives* that impact to be. In other words, in added-value selling, we must apply the benefit of the products and services we provide to helping the customer meet the nine critical needs of business.

In the following section, we will look at each of the nine needs in depth and pose questions for salespeople and their managers to determine if each need is a value product that we can or do provide our customers. As an important note, none of us will address all nine. Typically, we will find three or four that will pertain most directly to us.

THE NINE CRITICAL NEEDS OF BUSINESS

1. Product

Every business needs a product or service to sell. It may purchase a product for distribution or resale; it may buy components that integrate into other products; it may purchase raw materials. In the service industries, the "product" sold may be created from information or data sources or specialized knowledge.

A vendor provides value when it provides quality product or materials that the customers can successfully resell or that directly and clearly improve the customers' final product and enhance their competitive position. Value is further provided when there is a clear and measurable benefit to the business's customers.

> **Questions:**
> **1. Do we provide our customers a product, service, or component for resale?**
> **2. How important is *our* product to our customer's success?**
> **3. Does the customer see it this way?**

2. Funding

Sources of money are certainly a critical need. No business can survive for long without the availability of funds in order to operate, grow, and invest in the future. The most direct source of funds is from sales. Additionally, a business may access or leverage funds from loans, stock offerings, investments, payment terms, and similar sources.

> **Questions:**
> 1. Do we provide our customers a direct source of business funding through loans, payment terms, or other means?
> 2. Do our products and services significantly leverage sales for this customer?
> 3. Does the customer perceive this as important and a unique advantage of doing business with us?

3. Operations

Every business must operate. The basic tasks of selling, marketing, production, fulfillment, and administration must be carried out by people, technology, or some combination of the two. This may be as simple as the ability to make copies and answer the telephone or as complex as a national parts and service logistics system or operating a manufacturing line.

A vendor provides value when its product or service improves or streamlines operations to the direct benefit of the customer. It may make operation possible, more worry-free and reliable, less expensive or more efficient, or help the customer service its customers more effectively.

> **Questions:**
> 1. Do our customers perceive that our products or services significantly improve their operations?
> 2. Do the customers perceive that we have a positive impact on their ability to service the needs of their own customers better than their competition can?

4. Competitive Advantage

As we said earlier, some level of competitive advantage in the marketplace is necessary for any business to succeed and grow and to be considered a "going concern." Any element of competitive advantage provided by a vendor is value.

> **Question:**
> Do our customers perceive that our product or service provides them a unique source of competitive advantage in the marketplace?

5. Information

No business can work in a knowledge or information vacuum and expect to make business decisions that create market advantage. A successful enterprise requires a constant influx of information, such as sales, market, and financial data that can be provided from its internal operations or from any number of external sources.

> **Questions:**
> **1. Do we provide our customers specialized information or business knowledge that is not available from any other source?**
> **2. Do the customers see it this way?**

6. Expertise

Expertise is one of the most important elements of business success and competitive advantage in the marketplace. For example, every person hired by a company is hired for his or her expertise (or potential to gain that expertise). This is true whether the job title is CEO, Sales Manager, Sales Rep, Secretary, or Production Worker. Human resource departments conduct a continuous search for greater expertise.

Expertise can also be provided by consultants and vendors in any major business area: sales, marketing, production, administration, finance, and general management. These outside sources may provide expert advice or direction in their specific field as a primary product or as an element of an added-value program, for example, manufacturing methods, distribution channels, personnel selection, sales training and development, marketing, and other areas.

> **Questions:**
> **1. Do we provide our customers specialized business expertise that is not available from any other source?**
> **2. Do the customers see it this way?**

7. Customer Satisfaction

For success and long-term growth, satisfied customers who refer us to other customers are an absolute requirement. Vendors may influence their customers' customer satisfaction through the quality of the products and services they provide, as well as through added-value advice, knowledge, and support.

> **Question:**
> **Do our customers feel that our product or service plays a significant role in assuring the overall satisfaction of their customers?**

8. Profits

We've said it before: *Margin is the name of the game.* A vendor directly affects the customer's margin and ultimate profit picture through pricing and through services that enable the customer to control costs and/or achieve higher sales profitability.

Question:
Would the customers agree that we help them build maximum profits through our pricing, product quality, or added-value services?

9. Opportunity

Last and certainly not least, every business must have the "opportunity" to sell its products, usually in the form of sales leads, referrals, and repeat customers. A business generates its own opportunities through its sales and marketing activities. Likewise, vendors may generate opportunities for their customers through a variety of means, such as co-op marketing, joint selling, alliance programs, or brand recognition.

One example of this is the computer chip maker Intel Corporation's "Intel Inside" program which uses Intel's reputation as a tool to draw customer interest in its customers' products.

Question:
Do our customers perceive that we provide or enhance their opportunity to sell in the marketplace?

What about *sales*? Isn't that the tenth critical need?

I have been asked, "What about sales? Isn't that the most critical need of business?" My answer is a little bit "yes" and a little bit "no." True, a business without sales is not a successful business, but on the other hand, a business *with* sales is not necessarily a successful business either.

I deliberately left sales off the list simply because this seems to be where everyone starts when the question is asked "What are the most critical needs of business?" Sales are actions, events, *results*. Sales that are unprofitable or result in unsatisfied customers actually damage the business.

Good sales are the direct result of successfully meeting the nine critical needs of business.

EVALUATING NEEDS AND PERCEIVED VALUE

Real value is the direct result of the customers' *perception* of the significance of our impact on helping them meet their critical needs, and a sale is the result of how well we sell our value products.

Most vendors, who consider themselves to have high competitive advantage and low vulnerability to competitive intrusion, will strongly affect three or four of the nine criteria with their customers with a high perception level of value. In contrast, those who address only one or two needs or whose customers do not directly see them as high-value providers will have significantly less sales advantage and tend to be far more vulnerable to competitive intrusion.

The following format is a tool for evaluating exactly where a company stands in terms of the value it provides, the customer needs it can address, and what the customers think. It is an effective tool for evaluating marketplace perception, as well as individual customers. It is an even better tool for planning and coaching sales tactics.

FIGURE 5.4. EVALUATION TOOLS

CRITICAL BUSINESS NEEDS ANALYSIS

Market Strength

STEP 1: For which of the following critical business needs do we provide value to our customers?

- Product   How: _____
- Funding   How: _____
- Operations   How: _____
- Competitive Advantage   How: _____
- Information   How: _____
- Expertise   How: _____
- Customer Satisfaction   How: _____
- Profits   How: _____
- Opportunity   How: _____

Total number of criteria affected (market strength): _____

(CONTINUED ON NEXT PAGE)

CRITICAL BUSINESS NEEDS ANALYSIS

Market Perceived Value

STEP 2: Evaluate customer perception/rating of provided value importance to them.

Would customers say that they recognize each Value Product that we provide to them as: 5 = Critical for success, 4 = Moderately important, 3 = Somewhat important, 2 = Not very important, 1 = Unimportant or not recognized

- Product   Score: _____   Reason:_____

- Funding   Score: _____   Reason:_____

- Operations   Score: _____   Reason:_____

- Competitive Advantage   Score: _____   Reason:_____

- Information   Score: _____   Reason:_____

- Expertise   Score: _____   Reason:_____

- Customer Satisfaction   Score: _____   Reason:_____

- Profits   Score: _____   Reason:_____

- Opportunity   Score: _____   Reason:_____

Total Score: _____

What does it all mean?

Step 1 of the Critical Needs Analysis gauges overall market, segment, or customer strength, depending upon whether the analysis has been done for the marketplace, industry segment, or a specific customer. Generally speaking, the more critical business needs of customers that an organization knows it directly addresses (that is, providing customers specific value), the greater the sales organization's *potential* competitive strength.

Many sales and marketing groups unfortunately stop at this point. For some reason we assume that the customers should know how important we are to them. After all, haven't we made every effort to meet their requirements? To fulfill their needs? Remember that recent customer satisfaction survey? The customers are pretty happy! Therefore they *must* perceive our value.

It is a mistake to assume that the customer recognizes or clearly understands how a supplier's products and services directly affect one or more of the nine critical business needs. It's a fairly safe bet, however, that whatever their perception is, it is less than what we think it is or should be. In completing Step 2 of the analysis, it is probably wise and more accurate to reduce each perception score by 1 or even more.

FIGURE 5.5. CHARTING VALUE AND STRENGTH

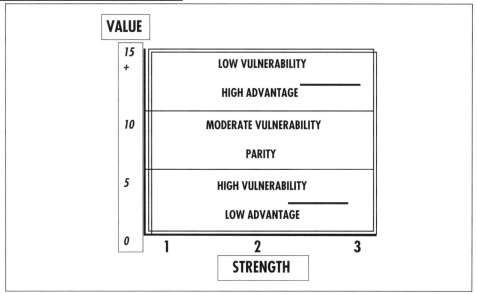

Mapping the results against the chart illustrates the overall competitive position held. A score between 1 and 5 indicates a low level of competitive advantage and a high vulnerability to competitive intrusion. It further indicates the vendor is viewed as a *replaceable commodity*. This would be a typical positioning for a company that sells primarily based on price. If the single need we address is primarily *increased profits* by providing the lowest price (strength of 1)—and the customer recognizes we are the lowest price provider (score of 5)—we understand and accept that we are highly vulnerable to a lower priced competitor.

On the other hand, if we, as a *value-focused* sales organization, believe that we meet three or more critical needs (for example, customer satisfaction, competitive advantage, and knowledge—strength of 3+), but our customer's perception is a 1 (unimportant or not recognized—score of 3), then our expensive added-value efforts are no more advantageous than if we simply cut prices. Customers who score their vendors at this level are not only willing to listen to a competitor's presentation, but also they will periodically seek out the other vendors to be sure they're "getting the best deal." At this level, a sales organization's marketing strategy must be to accept losses and gain more new accounts than it loses.

Scoring 6 to 10 indicates moderate vulnerability and general competitive parity. While generally not dissatisfied or looking for other vendors, customers who perceive their vendor's value in this range will generally be willing to at least listen to a competitor's sales pitch, particularly if they have a strong marketing angle. Competitive parity is perhaps the most difficult position to hold because vendors become *reactive* to the market and competition rather than *proactive* in their efforts to pull ahead of their competitors.

A good example of sales organizations that fall into these two categories are long-distance telephone services that sell virtually identical products and market fundamentally on price.

Scoring 11 or more shows a high level of competitive advantage and low vulnerability or "competition-proofing." These customers clearly understand how a vendor's products and value products help them successfully address specific and multiple critical business needs. At this level, the vendor is perceived as a *necessary business partner*. Most important, the customers believe that separation from that vendor could potentially *damage* their business.

These customers can be developed and grown for maximum sales and are unlikely even to be willing to look at the competition. A customer that is a "partner" not only provides the best additional business opportunity but also, because it is "competition-proofed," frees the vendor's sales organization to seek new customers without constantly firefighting or reselling every time a competitor makes a call on the customer. Additionally, vendors whose key customers are partners are typically *proactive* in the marketplace; that is, they are able to drive the market direction instead of only responding to competitor's sales and marketing programs and new features.

FIGURE 5.6. VALUE: PARTNER OR COMMODITY?

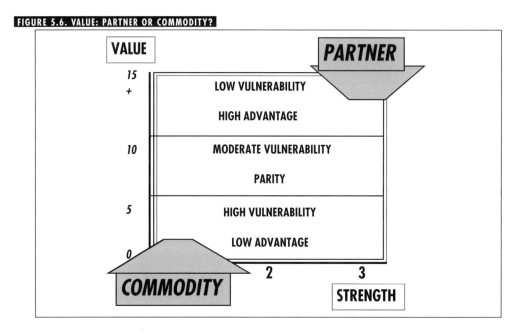

In summary, the real value of the Critical Business Needs Analysis is in helping a sales organization reposition or map the value products it offers against the true needs of customers, taking a hard look at customer perceptions and understanding exactly what these perceptions mean to an organization's competitive advantage and vulnerability.

Before anything else, the first and most important step in winning any new sales opportunity or improving any existing customer relationship is to identify the critical business needs, select the value products that can be provided, honestly evaluate the prospect/customer's perceptions, and develop a plan of action to strengthen those perceptions.

TARGETING COMPETITIVE VULNERABILITY

Looking carefully at our customer's perceptions of the value products we provide them has tremendous worth in developing a strategy for competitive advantage. However, it is also useful and potentially even more valuable as a tool for targeting *competitive vulnerability*.

The technique is the same, except that we complete the Critical Business Needs Analysis from the competitor's point of view. What is the customer's perception of how a competitor will meet his or her needs? What set of value products is the competitor offering, and how are *they* perceived by the customer?

For example, another vendor may be competing with us primarily on a small price advantage. (This addresses the profit need and is scored a 4 in the eyes of the customer.) Additionally, the competitor has general product feature parity. (For the purposes of this example, we'll assume it addresses operations and is scored a 3 as essentially equal to ours.) So the competitor scores a 7—equal and slightly better than our position based on only these two categories.

Using this information, we can develop a framework for a competitive strategy. Since we cannot control product features and are unwilling to reduce our price and profit margin, it's unlikely we will be able to leverage "Profit" or "Operations" enough to establish clear advantage. Previously we might have attempted to rely on "salesmanship" or personal relationship skills to sway the sale. We will be far better served, however, by evaluating the other critical business needs we can address that we know are *not a strength of the competitor*. We then develop a strategy to "sell" this unique value to the prospect. In other words, we identify and attack the competitor's vulnerability. We do not attack the competitor's strength head on, nor do we attack in areas where we have no real advantage.

This approach "changes the field of play" by competing on the right playing field where we have the home-team advantage and where the competition is not even aware the game is in progress.

When we discuss the sales methodology, STRATEGY MAPPING™, in the next chapter, we will introduce a condensed value analysis form as part of the worksheets for planning the sales territory, major accounts, and the sales opportunity.

Finally, here are some thoughts for "value-selling" managers:

- Use the Critical Business Needs Analysis as both a planning and territory/account review tool.
- Refocus sales representatives on understanding *real* customer needs and developing sales messages that present your products and services as real value.
- Develop sales strategies and planned sales activities around strengthening customers' value perceptions.
- Develop "vulnerability targets" by assessing the competitor's value position as well as your own!
- Assure that a viable BEST/NEXT strategy is always in place for every active sales opportunity.

SALES MANAGERS' PERSPECTIVES

JUSTIFYING OUTSIDE SALES REPS

Why do we have outside sales reps? The answer most managers give is, "to sell product." The problem is that sales reps and sales calls are expensive. No wonder so many companies are turning to less costly channels: telesales, catalogs, and resellers. So what's the future for outside sales?

We need to redefine the sales rep's job and make sure that the salespeople understand why they have a job!

The purpose of the Outside Sales Rep

"To provide a unique source of competitive advantage in the marketplace!"

That "redefinition" says clearly that the job of an outside sales rep is to create a unique source of competitive advantage in the marketplace that cannot be developed through other channels. That competitive advantage translates into three critical functions:

1. Establish working personal business relationships with customers that develop long-term repeat business.
2. Develop in-depth customer knowledge to enable the best servicing of customer needs and expectations.
3. Deliver unique added-value in addition to the product.
4. Deliver a revenue volume at a profit level that justifies the expense.

Another reminder that outside sales cannot be "discount selling"; it is "full price" selling justified by added-value.

CHAPTER 6

STRATEGY MAPPING™ — A SALES METHODOLOGY FOR OPPORTUNITY MANAGEMENT

STRATEGY MAPPING™ is an opportunity management sales methodology to resolve the M.A.Z.E. It stands on its own as a selling methodology, but as we shall see, it is particularly powerful when supported by sales automation technology. (A special note: STRATEGY MAPPING is not a sales automation software program. It is a new methodology that was specifically designed to take advantage of modern selling technologies and to be easily integrated into many or most SFA packages.)

STRATEGY MAPPING enables salespeople to assess sales territories, key accounts, and opportunities and "map" the *shortest route to the close* with the least backtracking to get back on course and by hitting the fewest dead ends. Further, it provides sales managers with an effective set of tools to assist salespeople in the planning processes and to coach sales performance. Remember that the goal of selling is to *increase sales cycles*!

FIGURE 6.1. INCREASE SALES CYCLES

Selling is not "closing."

Selling is increasing "*Completed Sales Cycles!*"

In the sales process management model, we saw how managing with sales progress milestones using sales automation technology could help managers continuously evaluate sales activities and effectiveness and thus improve general sales quality and execution. Tracking progress is fine when everything is going well, when the sales rep has a working, viable sales strategy in place, and the sale just seems to happen naturally. It's too bad that things aren't usually quite that easy in the real world.

From a manager's perspective, just having a way to know about potential sales problems and to track opportunity progress is a significant advance in its own right. For example, using SFA technology, a manager should be able to easily create something as simple as a pipeline report, showing each opportunity, milestone reached, and date — and drill down for more detailed opportunity data for greater analysis.

FIGURE 6.2. SAMPLE PIPELINE REPORT

PIPELINE REPORT

REP	ACCOUNT	OPPORTUNITY	MILESTONE	LAST ACTIVITY	FORECAST
TJM	Superior	Widget Project	Demo	2/1/96	90%
WWL	Flexo Int'l	SFA Project	Proposal	2/26/96	50%
YJH	American Co	Upgrade	Qualify	3/9/96	70%

But that's only the start. The manager's job has two totally *interdependent* tasks. Achieving one without the other is pointless:

1. Knowing what's going on
2. Knowing the absolutely best thing to do about it

Doing both of these effectively relies on technology as well as on experience and sales expertise. But to really work well, there need to be *integrated methodologies and processes* for planning and assessment that cover the total scope of the selling effort. That scope includes managing a territory and/or major accounts, opportunity management, and face-to-face selling. Together they create a framework for both the salesperson and the manager to make higher quality sales decisions, called STRATEGY MAPPING.

THE FIVE LEVELS OF STRATEGY MAPPING METHODOLOGIES

STRATEGY MAPPING for opportunity management is made up of five tiers or levels that come together into a single, cohesive selling tool, the STRATEGY MAP. The five levels are:

1. Sales Process Milestones
2. Value Product Selling
3. INFINITE SELLING™
4. THE STRATEGY MAP™
5. VISION SELLING™

As discussed earlier, *sales process milestones* (what's going on?) are the beginning or the first level of the sales process. Behind them lies the next tier or level, *value product selling*, the second level of the sales process, in which we defined the value component of the competitive advantage that we bring to the marketplace.

In this chapter, we will look at *INFINITE SELLING* and the sales *STRATEGY MAP*, the third and fourth levels of the sales process, a set of strategic and tactical planning methodologies that help us further refine the sales process into a more usable tool. In examining these levels, we'll discover more about developing BEST/NEXT strategies and tactics. Finally, we will look at *VISION SELLING*, the fifth level of the sales process, that ties everything together into the sales call.

It's one thing to say we need a defined sales process and a strategy methodology; it's quite another thing to have one. The following elements of STRATEGY MAPPING propose process models and strategic methodologies for salespeople and managers that can form the backbone for an organization's specific selling environment and style. Without these kinds of processes, sales managers have little or no framework upon which to base coaching.

INFINITE SELLING — A SALES PROCESS MODEL

The new role of management, combined with the new sales focus of building profitable customer relationships using value products must be supported by an equally new sales process model that supports both the sales manager and the sales representative.

FIGURE 6.3. THE INFINITE SELLING MODEL

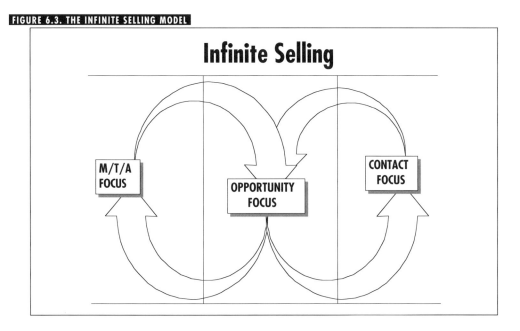

As indicated in Figure 6.3, the INFINITE SELLING sales process uses an *infinity loop* to illustrate the sequence in which salespeople must address the three basic and necessary "focuses" of selling and how these focuses logically flow from one to the other to produce maximum sales results:

1. The M/T/A, or Market/Territory/Account, focus
2. The Opportunity focus
3. The Contact focus

Taken together INFINITE SELLING creates a business framework for the total job of selling:

1. Building a market business plan
2. Managing and developing a sales territory
3. Key account management
4. Opportunity management: working and winning the sales opportunity or "deal"
5. Contact management: one-on-one selling

The logic of INFINITE SELLING is the integration and interdependence of the three focuses. Taken together, they enable a salesperson to build a successful, short- and long-term market position of competitive advantage.

The following illustration and subsequent explanation show how the three focuses of INFINITE SELLING tie together a very simple sample model of sales process milestones ("Find, Qualify, Develop, Solve, Close, Deliver, and Find More Opportunities") with specific sales activity modes and sales events.

INFINITE SELLING™ MODEL

Sales Milestones: 1. Find, 2. Qualify, 3. Develop, 4. Solve, 5. Close, 6. Deliver, 7. Find more opportunities

Focus	Cycle Step	Activity Mode	Events
M/T/A	FIND	PLANNING	Develop Personal Business Plan Develop Market and Territory Plan Develop Major Account Plans
		MARKETING	Conduct Market Analysis Create Strategy Execute Campaign Receive/Distribute Leads Find Opportunity
OPPORTUNITY Profile/Assessment (Loop 1)	QUALIFY	FACT-FINDING	Develop Opportunity • stated needs/pain • decision process/time • competitive position • power structure • product fit
		PLANNING	Go/No Go Decisions Design Opportunity Sales Plan • strategies/tactics • identify sales team/resources • target key contacts
CONTACT	DEVELOP	FACT-FINDING	Develop Influencer/Contacts Profiles • buyer roles • contact needs/pain • competitive position • decision criteria
		PLANNING	Develop Contacts Sales Plans • strategies for agreement • plan tactics ("To Do")
	SOLVE	EXECUTE PLAN	Sales Calls • presentation • demonstration

CONTINUED ON NEXT PAGE

Focus	Cycle Step	Activity Mode	Events
	CLOSE	EXECUTE PLAN	Close Contact for Support
			• handle objections
OPPORTUNITY	SOLVE	PROPOSAL	Presentation
(Loop 2)			• proposal delivery
	CLOSE	CONTRACTS	Contract Negotiation
			Order Placed
	DELIVER	IMPLEMENTING	Satisfaction Achieved
M/T/A	FIND	MARKETING	Search for New Opportunities
(return)			• leveraged by success

For this example we have used a simplified sales process or cycle similar to those used in typical selling methodologies. The specific process steps are:

1. **Find.** *In M/T/A focus*, develop a market business plan, territory plan, and key account plans, if applicable. Seek and identify high potential accounts and suspect sales opportunities that can be pursued.

2. **Qualify.** *In Opportunity focus*, assess and assure the sales opportunity meets qualification criteria — need defined, decision process known, funding allocated or available, product fit, competitive position. Develop an "Opportunity Sales Plan" to pursue. Evaluate the resources required (time, personnel, expense).

3. **Develop.** *In Contact focus*, identify and qualify contacts in the decision cycle, buyer decision-making roles, your competitive position, and agreements that need to be achieved with each contact to attain the prospect's support in the final decision. Develop planned tactics to address selling individual contacts.

4. **Solve.** *In Contact focus*, begin sales calls, specifically calls on contacts for the express purpose of closing for their support for your selection in the final decision.

5. **Close opportunity.** *Return to Opportunity focus*. When sufficient contact agreements have been achieved, you focus on the final proposal delivery, contract negotiation, and closing of the sales opportunity.

6. **Deliver.** *In Opportunity focus*, successful delivery and/or implementation of product or service and assured customer satisfaction.

7. **Find.** *Returning to M/T/A focus*, leverage the success of the sales opportunity to seek additional sales opportunities within the same account or other accounts in the territory.

We can also look at this process from the focus orientation perspective.

Step 1: M/T/A Orientation.

Begin at the left side of the infinity loop (see Figure 6.3). The sales cycle or milestone step is Find. Basic Activity Modes are Planning and Marketing with associated "Events" resulting in the production of a lead (or opportunity). The specific events could be performed by marketing, cold calling, telesales, direct mail, and other means.

Step 2: Opportunity Orientation (first loop).

At the center of the infinity loop, the salesperson is actively working with an identified opportunity. In this orientation, the cycle step will be to Qualify the opportunity *first* in a Fact-finding mode to develop an "Opportunity Profile" and *second* in the Planning mode to make the "Go/No Go" decision and develop an "Opportunity Sales Plan."

With a plan and clearer identification of the decision makers and decision criteria, the salesperson moves to Contact Orientation to begin the one-on-one selling process.

Step 3: Contact Orientation.

At the right-hand side of the infinity loop, the salesperson focuses on understanding the needs and requirements of the buying influencers (Contacts), presenting solutions, and "closing" each contact for his or her support in the decision process. The sales rep works primarily in Contact Orientation. The milestone steps are Develop, Solve, and Close. Events include developing "Contact/Influencer Profiles," "Contact/Influencer Sales Plans," presenting, demonstrating, gaining agreement, and closing.

Step 4: Opportunity Orientation (second loop).

Returning back to the center of the infinity loop, the salesperson goes back to working primarily in the Opportunity Orientation. The agreement of key buying influencers has been obtained, and the salesperson is prepared to Solve the opportunity in a Proposal or presentation that meets the needs of all buying influencers. The basic cycle steps are *Opportunity* Solve, Close, and Deliver. The last event in this step is "Customer Satisfaction Achieved," which returns us to the original step.

Step 5: M/T/A Orientation (return).

We have gone through the infinity loop and returned to where we began. Now we are looking for new or additional opportunities within this Account or in the Sales Territory. In the INFINITE SELLING model, *each time we complete a loop successfully, we increase our competitive strength and/or potential to do business with a given account.*

In summary, the INFINITE SELLING model creates a possible sales process workflow that illustrates the critical nature and powerful use of the three orientations to find new accounts; successfully identify, assess, work, and strategize opportunities; and sell more effectively to decision makers by creating better contact strategies and tactics within a new opportunity and account framework. But even more than this, the INFINITE SELLING progression illustrates the most fundamental and necessary goal of selling:

> **The successful sale is the one that is a springboard to more sales opportunities!**

The INFINITE SELLING model is the sales process path to that goal. We'll now take a more in-depth look at the three focuses.

THE MARKET/TERRITORY/ACCOUNT FOCUS

The Market/Territory/Account focus of INFINITE SELLING is perhaps the most important and critical step in the professional selling process because it sets the direction for the entire selling effort to follow. Many, if not all, salespeople naturally want to "get out there and sell"; that is, they want to make great sales calls, follow up leads, give sales presentations, and in short, go right into *execution*, in the belief that sales will result from their efforts.

FIGURE 6.4. THE M/T/A FOCUS

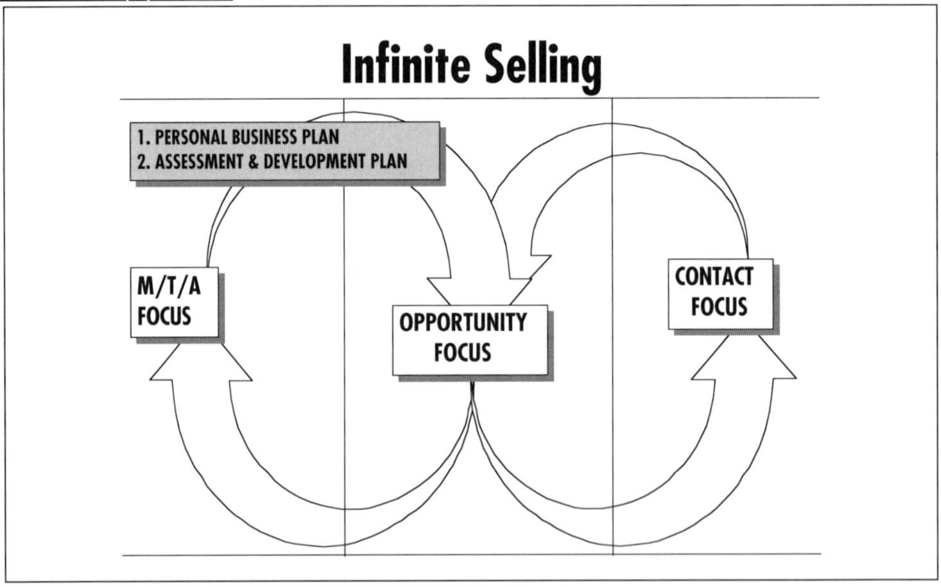

Infinite Selling

1. PERSONAL BUSINESS PLAN
2. ASSESSMENT & DEVELOPMENT PLAN

M/T/A FOCUS

OPPORTUNITY FOCUS

CONTACT FOCUS

It's not enough, however, just to make "great" sales calls. The real task is to determine *which great sales calls to make*! The "right" great sales calls are those with the greatest potential for success that can be achieved with the least effort and expenditure of resources. If we do not take the time to find and identify these, in one way or another, we end up "smokestacking."

The M/T/A focus is really the creation of a salesperson's **Personal Business Plan**: setting realistic goals, assessing and identifying territory potential and key account prospects, planning necessary resources to meet anticipated selling obstacles, and evaluating the personal effort and tasks necessary to achieve these goals.

The process begins with the M/T/A focus (Market/Territory/Account), specifically building the following plans:

1. Personal Market Business Plan/Territory Analysis
2. Account Assessment and Development Plan

THE PERSONAL MARKET BUSINESS PLAN AND TERRITORY ANALYSIS

Every salesperson is a business in his or her own right. Like any business, success is measured by the salesperson's ability to go to market—namely, to sell products and services, recognize revenue, and realize a profit in the form of salary, base, bonus, or commissions. Salespeople need to develop this view of themselves, as well as the view of their company as their investor who must receive a fair return on investment. What is the job of the sales manager in this view? He or she is the *Territory Banker* who manages and protects the investment by helping assure the sales rep's success.

Like any business then, a salesperson needs a *business plan*—and every sales manager must assure that every sales rep has one in place before he or she heads out into the marketplace to do business. As every banker knows:

> **The best predictor of business success or failure
> is the business plan!**

On the average, a company invests between $80,000 and $150,000 each year to put an outside salesperson "on the road," which does not include commissions or bonuses paid. What banker would invest that amount of money without a clear, high-probability business plan in place? Yet, as companies, we do it all the time. Besides, what sales manager would not rather know at the beginning of the year if his or her salespeople had *viable* plans in place to make quota rather than wait to find out at the end of the year that they didn't?

Essentially the salesperson's "personal business plan" contains five major elements:

1. The **physical characteristics** of the sales territory: demographics, potential, accessibility, competitive position, reference base, history, and so forth.
2. A **competitive assessment:** the competition's strengths, weaknesses, and strategies; the value perception of their customers, and competitive vulnerability targets.
3. A **strengths and weakness assessment:** a critical look at the company and its prod-

ucts, including an analysis of the company's overall value perception in the marketplace and in key accounts or customers.

4. **Goals and Objectives:** the market position and the sales metrics the salesperson plans to achieve, such as account penetration, revenue goals, target accounts, or product mix.

5. The **investment:** what it will take in terms of time, money, personal effort, and other resources to achieve sales and market goals.

THE **STRATEGY MAP** BUSINESS PLANNING METHODOLOGY

In business planning for the Market/Territory, Major Accounts, and Sales Opportunities, we are going to use a consistent, logical business planning methodology that addresses each of the five elements of a successful business plan. This methodology is illustrated in a sample "Territory and Market Planner" later in this chapter.

The STRATEGY MAP business planning methodology is based on four criteria for effectiveness:

1. **Workable.** The techniques must reflect *how* we want our people to sell in their specific marketplaces, including the factors we feel are important to their success.

2. **Executable.** More than just a planning or thinking exercise, the personal plans of the salespeople must be "strategic" plans that they can develop and turn into executable sales tactics and actions.

3. **Usable.** Techniques and methods need to be simple and easy to remember so that they can be used daily without complex forms or constant reference to manuals. Key plan information — especially the account and opportunity plans — should be able to be included in our sales automation database for easy reference and updating so that current plan data can be shared with management and others who may need it (support, marketing).

4. **Coachable.** The planning system must work for managers as well as salespeople. It should facilitate joint planning and sales progress review to consistently assure that the salespeople are executing the optimal sales tactics.

STRATEGY MAPPING will meet each of these criteria.

FIGURE 6.5. OVERVIEW OF BUSINESS PLAN METHODOLOGY

The STRATEGY MAP business plan is a five-step process that guides the salesperson from looking at long-term goals, to examining more immediate short-term or current-year objectives, and ultimately to developing executable sales strategies and tactics to achieve those goals. The result is a focused and realistic road map to success that reduces or eliminates many of the pitfalls of the M.A.Z.E.

1. Long-Term Goals. Typically, these are a one- to three-year view of objectives for revenue attainment, territory development, and other objectives, as illustrated in Figure 6.6.

FIGURE 6.6. BUSINESS PLAN: LONG-TERM OBJECTIVES

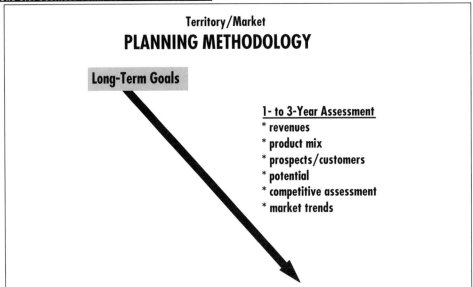

Examples of long-term goals may include territory revenue or new account growth goals; product-line revenue, mix, or growth; establishment of competitive advantage or attaining leadership in a specific market niche; and personal goals.

"Personal goals" might include earnings, promotion or advancement, or skill development. It is also worthwhile to use this section of the plan to consider nonbusiness personal goals, for example, lifestyle (car, home, and other possessions) investment, future financial needs (college tuition), retirement, desire to relocate to another geographical area, and so forth. For many people, these nonbusiness goals are their true motivators. In other words, their success in work is only a means to achieve their personal goals.

2. Short-Term Objectives. The short-term objectives are almost identical to the process for the long-term objectives, with the obvious difference that they refer to the current or upcoming sales year. Typically, revenue goals and product mix are planned by quarters. Key accounts are targeted for short-term growth or penetration and immediate competitive issues are addressed.

FIGURE 6.7. BUSINESS PLAN: SHORT-TERM OBJECTIVES

Personal goals are important at this level of planning, as well as a source of personal motivation to work for tangible results of success. Some years ago, I worked for an excellent manager, Phil, who managed and motivated his salespeople exclusively through personal goals. At the beginning of each sales year, Phil had each salesperson select a tangible "reward," which he or she would buy at the end of the year if the goal had been achieved. He also had each one sign a letter committing to this plan. For some, the reward was a boat, car, vacation home, or golf clubs. For others, it was an increased bank balance or investments. Phil also had each person frame a picture of his or her goal and prominently display it in the office. Throughout the year, Phil managed his people through these personal goals. Imagine the feelings of the salesperson who didn't achieve the goals at the end of the year when everyone one else was showing off his or her personal rewards!

In short, a smart manager makes personal goals as important in planning as business goals.

3. **Resources Available.** What resources are currently available to help us make long- and short-term goals? These resources may include territory demographics, time, personal skills, market position, product, support, money, or even customer value perception.

FIGURE 6.8. BUSINESS PLAN: RESOURCES

Territory/Market
PLANNING METHODOLOGY

Resources

Resources Available
* Demographics/access
* Skills & knowledge
* Information
* Support
* Financial
* Competitive vulnerability
* Product/pricing
* Perceived value

Resources are many and varied. For example, a sales territory with many installed accounts and a large amount of potential for new or additional business is clearly a resource. The expense budget is also a resource, as are personal selling skills. In other words, these resources are the available "tools" of selling.

4. **Obstacles Anticipated.** What obstacles to success do we expect to encounter for which we can plan in advance? Resources and obstacles are often two sides of the same coin. For example, the demographics of our territory can be viewed as a resource if the territory is filled with active accounts and a great potential for sales opportunities. Conversely, it can be viewed as an obstacle if it is undeveloped with few reference accounts and is geographically dispersed.

FIGURE 6.9. BUSINESS PLAN: OBSTACLES

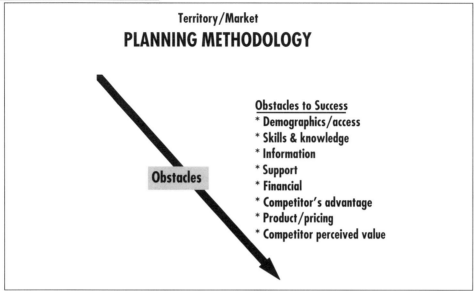

5. Tactics Planned. *Tactics* is defined as "the application of resources to obstacles to achieve objectives." In other words, we can only overcome the obstacles we may face in the selling process with the resources we have at hand. So how do we plan to use those resources most effectively?

FIGURE 6.10. BUSINESS PLAN: TACTICS

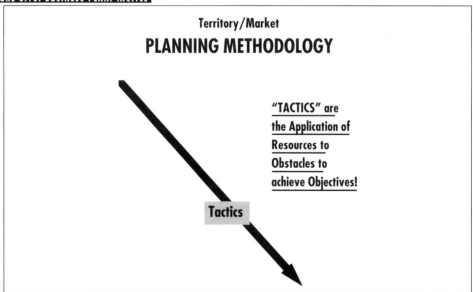

Given the obstacle of an undeveloped territory, what can we do to change this situation by utilizing the resources at hand (which are all we have!)? Should we spend marketing or expense dollars on a direct-mail campaign or on travel to make sales calls? Should we conduct seminars and bring in a corporate speaker? Or, from another perspective, should we invest time and money in education to improve our personal skills or industry knowledge to increase our sales effectiveness? In summary, we need tactics to address each obstacle and make the best use of our limited available resources.

6. **Requirements.** What do we need that we don't already have? As we created tactics to address obstacles, our plans may have identified obstacles that we do not believe we can overcome with the current resources at hand. We can make a business case for additional resources. If that's not possible, we must revise our tactics to accommodate our plans and allocate resources differently.

FIGURE 6.11. BUSINESS PLAN: REQUIREMENTS

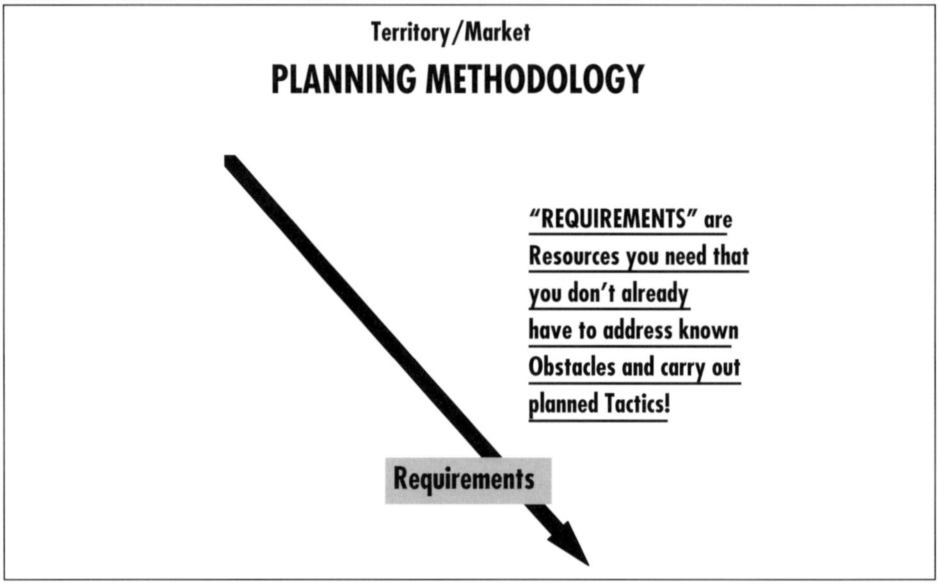

Territory/Market
PLANNING METHODOLOGY

"REQUIREMENTS" are Resources you need that you don't already have to address known Obstacles and carry out planned Tactics!

Requirements

For example, after completing a business plan, a salesperson may review his or her strategy with management. In that presentation, the rep shows the manager that much of the new account potential in the territory is in a specific industry (for example, insurance, banking, high-tech manufacturing). To penetrate those accounts effectively, the salesperson recommends a targeted direct-mail campaign, which is not in the budget or plan for the upcoming year.

There are three possible results of this scenario. First, the manager agrees with the sales rep's business case and approves the additional resources or tries to help the salesperson get them by moving the request to senior management with a strong recommendation. Second, the manager agrees with the plan but must tell the rep that no additional resources are available. Third, the manager disagrees with the plan. In the second and third scenarios, the manager is effectively telling the salesperson that he or she must come up with a different set of tactics to achieve the same goals, *using the resources at hand.*

Helping salespeople develop these kinds of winning, realistic tactics and requirements is a critical task of sales managers. As managers, it is our responsibility to assure that the plans with which our people go to market are, in fact, achievable.

The result of this business planning process is a clear definition of our plan for success in the marketplace. The challenges are clearly defined, as well as the tactics and requirements necessary to overcome them.

This kind of business planning, done at the beginning of the sales year, can significantly change the way managers regard their salespeople and the way in which they manage them. For example, a well-developed STRATEGY MAP business plan tells a manager exactly how the sales rep is going to go about making his or her goals this year. The manager's tasks are to assess how realistic and achievable those goals are and to assist the salesperson in fine-tuning them. Then the manager bases how he or she coaches the rep throughout the year by using the final plan.

A secondary benefit, although it may not seem so at first, is the "No-Go Business Plan." In this case, despite the best efforts of the salesperson and the manager, no one can develop a business plan that can achieve the assigned goals, for example, the sales quota for the new year. Although the result is frustrating, the benefit is that we have identified the problem at the beginning of the year, when it is still possible to do something about it, instead of well into the sales year when it is far too late.

Finally, the manager's role as territory banker comes into play again: "If you can't develop a workable business plan for success, then I can't invest in you this year!"

The following is a completed sample STRATEGY MAP for the first step or focus of INFINITE SELLING: the Territory and Market Planner.

STRATEGY MAPPING TERRITORY AND MARKET PLANNER

TERRITORY/MARKET ASSESSMENT:

A. Long-Term Goals (1 – 3 years)
"Long-term goals" requires the salesperson to take a three-year view of his or her sales territory, including estimates of future sales revenues and product quotas (if applicable).

Key accounts or prospects who have the potential to produce significant business over the three-year planning period are identified, as well as major competitors whom we can expect to encounter within this specific sales territory.

1. General Revenue Goals

1996	1997	1998
$1,200,000	$1,500,000	$1,750,000

2. Product-Line Revenue Goals

Product	1996	1997	1998
Product 1	400,000	500,000	1,000,000
Product 2	400,000	700,000	500,000
Product 3	400,000	300,000	250,000

3. Known Key Accounts/Prospects in Territory/Market

Account	Customer Y/N	Products	$ Potential	Competitor
1. Superior Industries	Y	1, 2, 3	$$ – long-term	Floppo
2. NewTech America	Y	2	12,000	none
3. Karma Int'l	N	3	50,000	Energex
4. Worldview, Inc.	N	2, 3	100,000	unknown
5. Shaw Services	Y	1	12,500	Floppo
6. Dart Technology	N	1	25,000	Floppo
7. Command Ind.	N	1, 2	50,000	Energex
8. Midwest, Inc.	Y	3	300,000	none
9. CRC	N	??		

4. Competition

Competitor	Strength	Weakness
1. Floppo	Price	Lack of support
2. Energex	Feature-rich	Reliability record

5. Personal Long-Term Goals

1. Income goals

2. Advancement and promotion

3. Personal goals

B. Short-Term Goals (current year)

"Short-term goals" focuses on the current or immediate upcoming sales year to be planned and may involve dollar revenues and/or unit volume product mix goals.

"Focus accounts" are those which we believe have a realistic revenue potential within the year or which must be developed in order to achieve sales goals.

1. Revenue Goals

1st Quarter	2nd Quarter	3rd Quarter	4th Quarter
$200,000	$300,000	$400,000	$300,000

2. Product-Line Revenue Goals

Product	Units	Revenue $
Product 1	10	800,000
Product 2	7	200,000
Product 3	5	200,000

3. 1996 Focus Accounts

Account	Opportunity	Revenue $	Active Y/N
1. Superior	Project A	500,000	N
2. CRC	Project B	600,000	N
3. Worldview	Project C	400,000	Y

4. Personal Short-Term Goals

1. This year's income goals

2. Make 100% Club

3. Be top unit sales rep

4. Develop business planning skills

C. Resource/Obstacle Assessment

This section identifies a group of typical factors that may be evaluated either as "resources" or as potential "obstacles" by the salesperson.

Resources Available to Make Short-Term Goals

Resources/Obstacles	Resource	Obstacle
Demographics (sufficient accounts/opportunities identified)		X
Territory Accessibility (ease of coverage)	X	
Personal Selling Skills (strong or weak)	X	
Product Knowledge (strong or weak)	X	
Business Development Skills (strong or weak)		X
Pre-Sales Support: technical (strong or weak)	X	
Pre-Sales Support: management (strong or weak)		X
Pre-Sales Support: marketing (strong or weak)		X
Post-Sale Support/Implementation	X	
Account Knowledge (industry, business goals, defined needs)		X
Account/Key Contact Access (decision makers)		X
Competitive Customer Base (satisfied or vulnerable)	X	
Competitive Marketing Presence (active or inactive)		X
Financial Resources (expense budget, etc.)	X	

For each "obstacle" identified above, the salesperson details the issues and a plan to address and resolve that obstacle — specifically by application of known resources.

D. Tactics/Requirements
(strategies to develop strengths and resolve obstacles)

Demographics (sufficient accounts/opportunities): Good territory but have not identified all potential accounts clearly. To accomplish this I will ... .

Territory Accessibility (ease of coverage): Generally good. Most accounts located in the major metros in my area. I can improve my coverage by ... .

Personal Selling Skills: Strong sales skills, but I need development in financial selling and cost justification. To accomplish this I will … .

Product Knowledge: Strong in product 1. Need more on product 3 and on competitor's new product. To get this I will … .

Business Development Skills: Need to improve overall large account planning by … .

Pre-Sales Support: Technical: Good. Can improve any deficiencies by … .

Pre-Sales Support: Management: Managers need to know better what the customers are saying and what is really going on. Can improve this by … .

Pre-Sales Support: Marketing: Need more support, new materials, etc. I can leverage this by … .

Post-Sale Support/Implementation: Good. Concerned that if goals are met, there may not be sufficient resources available. I can communicate this to … .

Account Knowledge (industry, business goals, defined needs): Need more info in the following areas … . I'll get info by … .

Account/Key Contact Access (decision makers): I will gain better selling access to higher level decision makers by … .

Competitive Customer Base: Competition's customer base is weak and unhappy. I will capitalize on this by … .

Competitive Marketing Presence: Weak now, but expect more soon. Plan to counter this by … .

Financial Resources: If additional dollars are needed to make goals, how will funds be invested/spent?

E. Marketplace Perceived-Value Analysis (Nine business needs)

For this specific territory or market, what is the overall value perception of our company's products and services in existing accounts and/or prospects? What are the primary value products we sell? Where do we need to improve? What is our competitive position?

Identify the three key value products that you believe you offer your customers, and evaluate the customers' perceptions of your importance to their business success.

Value ("We provide our customers … .")	Provided?	Perception
Product or Service for Resale		
Funding (sales, investment, terms, etc.)		
Operations (physical operation of the business)	X	3
Competitive Advantage — increase		
Customer Satisfaction — increase		
Information — uniquely available		
Expertise — not available internally	X	3
Profits — increase	X	2
Opportunity — increase sales opportunities		
	TOP 3 TOTAL	8

F. Territory Advantage/Vulnerability Position

Score	Position
11 – 15	High Competitive Advantage/Low Vulnerability to Competitive Intrusion
6 – 10 XX	Competitive Parity, No Perceived Advantage, Moderate Vulnerability
0 – 5	Competitive Disadvantage/High Vulnerability to Competitive Intrusion

G. Top Three "One-Point Plan"

In the "One-Point Plan," the salesperson defines his or her strategy to improve the rating of each "value product" by at least one point.

Detail strategy to improve "Top 3" selected value perceptions by 1 point:

I plan to improve perceptions of Operation, Expertise, and Profits in my territory by:

1. Marketing Plans

2. Customer Communications

   A. Direct sales calls

   B. Direct mail

   C. Other

3. Development of references

THE MAJOR ACCOUNT PLAN

The major account is the second part of the Territory/Market Plan. We have now identified high potential or target accounts that are part of our general business strategy. The next step is to evaluate and assess each "key" or "major" prospect account and develop a plan to penetrate or develop that business.

An important distinction is that this is a plan to assess and develop an *account* or *company*, not a specific sales opportunity. The need for a comprehensive account development plan is fairly obvious in the large-account environment. Large accounts are often a complex sell, and each account may offer many sales opportunities, either in its own right or within subsidiaries or other divisions.

For some salespeople and in some markets, however, an account and opportunity may appear to be the same thing. This is particularly true when we sell to smaller companies that may offer little potential for repeat business. Nonetheless, as in the large-account world where each sale leverages additional opportunities, each smaller account successfully added to our customer list provides leverage in the marketplace. In this case, we should focus on planning the companies and prospects who can, in fact, provide that same kind of leverage because of the industry they are in, or because of their reputation as an industry leader, or perhaps because of their potential for real success with our products and services.

MAJOR ACCOUNT PLAN

PART 1: KEY ACCOUNT PROFILE: SUPERIOR INDUSTRIES

The initial step in the major account plan is identification of the markets served and products sold by the account. An important assessment is to quantify account revenues by industry and markets and determine whether the company is growing, stable, or declining. This information is generally readily available from any number of commercial reference sources.

A. Industry

Industry	Market Served	$ Rev.	Position	Products
Precision widgets	Aeronautical	1.0M	G	Maxiwidget
	Automotive	5.4M	S	Miniwidget
Component Parts	Medical Equipment	12.0M	G	Widgetomometer
	Instrumentation	.5M	D	Weeniewidgets

Market Position: G = Growing, S = Stable, D = Declining

In this example, Superior Industries is a "widget" and component parts manufacturer serving multiple markets, two of which are growing and may point to the greatest long-term sales opportunities.

B. Corporate Organization

The "Corporate Organization" section identifies subsidiary, parent, or affiliate companies or divisions of a large account. Identified companies or divisions in this list should be assessed as potential leveraged prospects resulting from a completed sale to the profiled account.

Company	P/S/A/D	Location	Products	Position	Customer Y/N
Wally's Woodchips Int'l.	P	Keeokuk, ME	Woodchips	D	N
ABC Int'l.	A	Aurora, IL	Jet engines	G	N
Finex	S	Sheboygan, WI	Cables	S	Y
Superior Component	D	Merrimack, NH	Components	G	Y

P/S/A/D: P = Parent, S = Subsidiary, A = Affiliate, D = Division
Market Position: G = Growing, S = Stable, D = Declining

C. Key Contact Analysis

Who are the important decision-making contacts within this account who directly or indirectly may play a role in decisions affecting the sales of our products to this company? Are they personally known or unknown to us; that is, have we had direct contact with them? Do we have access to them during sales efforts?

What is their position regarding our company and products? Generally, are they a "Supporter" or "Open" or "Against"? A "Supporter" may be a satisfied customer or someone who is predisposed to favor our products and services. "Open" indicates our belief that the contact has no strong vendor preference. "Against" can indicate dissatisfaction with us or our products or that the contact generally prefers a specific competitor.

What role does each of these contacts generally play in sales decisions in which we are involved? Are they usually decision makers, do they significantly influence decisions? This information is often provided by our "Supporters" or from historical account data or experience. It may also be inferred from corporate organization charts (which can be misleading because title and decision-making power are not necessarily the same).

Contact	Title	Access Y/N	S/O/A	Role in Decisions
1. Marvin Marvin III	Chairman	N	O	Approver over $1M
2. Arthur Engles	VP Sales	Y	S	Influences decisions
3. Shelly Barman	Director	N	O	Final approval
4. Earl Beeman	Manager	Y	S	Evaluates
5. Max Wells	Engineer	Y	A	Evaluates and recommends

S/O/A: S = Support, O = Open, A = Against

D. Previous Sales Summary

Detail the history of recent sales to this account as well as the result and/or satisfaction issues.

Date	Product	Dept/Div.	$ Rev.	Result
1/95	Our Product	Manufacturing	100K	successful install
3/95	Upgrade	Manufacturing	10K	to resolve problem

PART 2: ACCOUNT DEVELOPMENT PLANNER: SUPERIOR INDUSTRIES

The account development plan is the second element of account planning. Except as noted, functionally it is identical to the territory/market plan we completed earlier and is based on the same business planning model of Long-Term Goals, Short-Term Objectives, Resources, Obstacles, Tactics, and Requirements.

KEY ACCOUNT: SUPERIOR INDUSTRIES

A. Long-Term Goals (1–3 years)

1. General Revenue Goals

1996	1997	1998
$300,000	$400,000	$500,000

2. Product-Line Revenue Goals

Product	1996	1997	1998
Product 1	150,000	200,000	250,000
Product 2	100,000	150,000	200,000
Product 3	50,000	50,000	50,000

3. Potential Long-Term Sales Opportunities In this Account

Opportunity	Active Y/N	Products	$ Potential	Competitor
1. Chicago facility	Y	Product 2	100,000	Floppo
2. New York facility	Y	Upgrade	20,000	none
3. Chicago	N	Product 3	25,000	unknown
4. Peoria	N	Product 1	50,000	Energex

4. Competition In this Account

Competitor	Strength	Weakness
1. Floppo	Lowest price	Limited support
2. Energex	Feature advantage	Proprietary technology

5. Other Long-Term Account Development Goals

1. Consulting and audit projects

2. Upgrade opportunity

3. Sell to component division

B. Short-Term Account Goals (current year)

1. Revenue Goals

1st Quarter	2nd Quarter	3rd Quarter	4th Quarter
$75,000	$100,000	$50,000	$75,000

2. Product-Line Revenue Goals

Product	Units	Revenue $
Product 1	25	250,000
Product 2	5	35,000
Product 3	80	15,000

3. 1996 Focus Sales Opportunities

Opportunity	Description	Revenue $	Active Y/N
1. Chicago	Product 1	100,000	Y
2. New York	Product 2 upgrade	20,000	Y
3. Cohasset	Product 3	50,000	N
4. Chicago	Product 2	50,000	N

4. Other Short-Term Account Development Goals

1. Establish solid relationship with decision makers

2. Prove we can support what we sell

3. Get introductions to other company facilities and divisions

C. Resource/Obstacle Assessment

Resources Available to Make Short-Term Goals

Resources/Obstacles	Resource	Obstacle
Potential (sufficient opportunities for sales investment)	X	
Account Accessibility (ease of coverage)		X
Personal Selling Skills		X
Product Knowledge (related to account industry/application)	X	
Account Development Skills		X
Pre-Sales Support: technical	X	
Pre-Sales Support: management	X	
Pre-Sales Support: marketing		X
Post-Sale Support: implementation	X	
Account Knowledge (industry, business goals, defined needs)		X
Account/Key Contact Access (decision makers)		X
Competitive Install/Customer Satisfaction	X	
Competitive Marketing Presence		X
Financial Resources (expense budget, etc.)	X	

D. Tactics/Requirements
(Strategies to develop strengths and resolve obstacles)

Potential (sufficient opportunities): Good potential in this account — enough to make short- and long-term goals. These need to be more specifically identified and better time frames established to make sure they are real.

Account Accessibility (ease of coverage): An obstacle — account locations are on the East Coast and in the Midwest. Going to require significant travel.

Personal Selling Skills: I have solid selling skills that work well with my technical contacts in this account. My executive-level presentation skills can use some development to take this account to the next level. To do this I will … .

Product Knowledge (customer industry/needs/application): Strong — solid industry knowledge, trends and direction, etc.

Account Development Skills: Need to be strengthened — especially account planning. To accomplish this I will … .

Pre-Sales Support: Technical: Excellent resource in place.

Pre-Sales Support: Management: Management needs to understand better what is happening in the field and what customers are saying. To do this we can … .

Pre-Sales Support: Marketing: Same as management. Also, we need marketing tools more up-to-date, easier accessibility. I suggest we … .

Post-Sale Support/Implementation: Strong, but if we meet account goals, we may stretch our ability to implement on time. Suggest we … .

Account Knowledge (industry, business goals, defined needs and process): I have generally good information, but it is a little out of date because of reorganizations in this account. To resolve this I will … .

Account/Key Contact Access (decision makers): Need to gain better access to the real decision makers. I have been blocked so far. To resolve this I will … .

Competitive Install and Customer Satisfaction: Need to find out more about how the competition is doing, who their supporters are, and develop a strategy. I will ... .

Competitive Marketing Presence: Unknown. Need to find out by ... .

Financial Resources: Good. I can meet goals with available finances. (Or: Inadequate. I need to request additional dollars which will be specifically used to ... .)

E. Account Perceived-Value Analysis (Nine business needs)

Value ("We provide this account ... .")	Provided?	Perception
Product or Service for Resale		
Funding (sales, investment, terms, etc.)		
Operations (physical operation of the business)	X	4
Competitive Advantage — increase		
Customer Satisfaction — increase		
Information — uniquely available		
Expertise — not available internally	X	2
Profits — increase	X	2
Opportunity — increase sales opportunities		
	TOP 3 TOTAL	8

F. Account Advantage/Vulnerability Position

Score	Position
11–15	High Competitive Advantage/Low Vulnerability to Competitive Intrusion
6–10 XX	Competitive Parity, No Perceived Advantage, Moderate Vulnerability
0–5	Competitive Disadvantage/High Vulnerability to Competitive Intrusion

G. Key Competitor Perceived-Value Analysis (Nine business needs)

In the account plan and the subsequent opportunity plan, we have added an additional element of a value analysis for one or more key competitors. The objective is to identify potential vulnerability targets.

Value ("They provide this account .... ")	Provided?	Perception
Product or Service for Resale		
Funding (sales, investment, terms, etc.)		
Operations (physical operation of the business)	X	3
Competitive Advantage — increase		
Customer Satisfaction — increase		
Information — uniquely available	X	3
Expertise — not available internally		
Profits — increase	X (cheaper)	4
Opportunity — increase sales opportunities		
	TOP 3 TOTAL	10

H. Competitor Vulnerability Targets

Value	Strategy
Expertise	We offer unique expertise that can improve profits. Sell this to ....

I. Top Three "One-Point Plan"

Detail strategy to improve "Top 3" selected value perceptions by 1 point:

I plan to improve this account's value perceptions of our Expertise, Operations, and Profits

by doing the following .... .

In the process of completing the Territory/Market Plan and the Account Plan, we have accomplished several goals key to sales success:

1. Identification and assessment—we have enough information on the territory and targeted accounts to make a realistic assessment of resources necessary to achieve goals and the overall viability of our plan.
2. We have specific plans and strategies in place to address anticipated sales obstacles, including the development of competitive vulnerability targets.
3. We have a *coachable* idea of where we're going and how we're going to get there.

THE OPPORTUNITY FOCUS

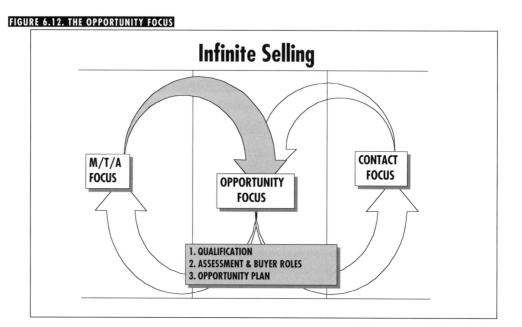

FIGURE 6.12. THE OPPORTUNITY FOCUS

In the excitement of a potential sale—particularly a *big* potential sale—it is too easy to rush ahead blindly and start making lots of sales calls. Before you know it, you're lost in the M.A.Z.E., thrashing through the deal without a solid plan or strategy, wasting time and resources.

If you think it only happens to rookies, I'll give you a real-life example of just how easily it happens. It's a true story.

I received a call from the Information Systems Manager of a Fortune 100 company who called "out of the blue" with a fantastic opportunity. He told me that he had read my book and that he was sure that I was the consultant they needed for an international sales force automation systems audit project, *to begin immediately*! The potential fee was around $100,000! That's enough to get your attention!

They needed me to fly out the next Tuesday to their corporate headquarters on the West Coast to make a one-hour presentation to the Sales VP and project team and to present a written proposal of my capabilities to complete a sales automation audit. All my questions would be answered then. (I should point out that I was expected to pay my own way, an investment on my part of probably $2,500. But for a $100K opportunity, that's not a lot, is it?)

Of course, I said, "Great!" There was a small problem because I was booked with another client that day (naturally the *only* day he said they could see me!). I assured him, however, that I was certain I could "move some things around on my calendar" and I would call him back later that day to confirm. That delay saved me.

After singing a few choruses of "We're in the Money!", the attack of "big deal euphoria" began to wear off, and I started to ask myself, "What was I really doing?"

I had promised to invest time and hard-earned money (and delay another project) for an opportunity I knew almost nothing about. My only justification was that the caller told me he thought I was wonderful and dangled a lot of money in front of me. (I was starting to feel like one of Pavlov's dogs.) That's when I made a list of all the things I didn't know:

1. What is the real scope of the project?
2. What are the client's expectations? Is it a fit with what I do or can do? What is driving the project (need!)? What is the problem that makes it worthwhile for them to invest $100,000? Can the project, as they view it, be successfully completed by *anyone*?
3. Is this something that I *want* to do? Is it a company that I am philosophically in alignment with? Do I like them?
4. Do I have competition? Did they really call me because I'm the one they really need, or are they just comparison shopping to validate another vendor?
5. Is this a real project that is already approved? Is the money for it already allocated? What's the time frame?
6. Does the person who *loves* me have the authority to select me? In other words, is he the decision maker?
7. If I travel to make this sales call, will it be the only trip at my expense, or will they expect me to come back several more times?

You might say that my mistake was that I ignored the sales basic of *qualifying*, but I maintain that I qualified initially as well as most salespeople would have in that situation. So what happened next?

I called them back the next morning, armed with my list of questions, to be told again that everything would be covered when I arrived. My contact, it turned out, couldn't answer any of the questions about scope or expectations. All he could tell me was that the decision would be made soon and that if I didn't come on that day, I would be dropped from consideration. And, by the way, the other two consultants he contacted were being more cooperative about coming out on short notice!

Well, that changed everything, didn't it? I'm not going anywhere on those terms. Still, for me it's a great object lesson. After twenty-five years of selling (and writing a book on how not to do this, for God's sake!), it painfully reminds me of the power of a "big deal" to completely disconnect the brain's selling logic circuits. Tell me I'm wonderful and that you want to give me a bunch of money and I'll follow you anywhere. At least I got a good story out of it, and it proves an axiom of opportunity management:

FIGURE 6.13. FIRST RULE OF OPPORTUNITY MANAGEMENT

THE 1st RULE OF OPPORTUNITY MANAGEMENT

"It's what you DON'T know that kills you!"

The Opportunity focus of the INFINITE SELLING process is an assessment and planning step. In assessment, we make the initial "Go, No Go" decision if we want to compete. Do we know everything we need to know to make the *early* evaluation of whether the deal can be won, and are we willing to invest what it will take to win? If the answer to each of these is "yes," it's time to develop a more detailed opportunity plan or STRATEGY MAP of the *fastest route to the close*.

OPPORTUNITY MANAGEMENT — ASSESSMENT AND PLANNING

The most difficult thing to do in selling is "walking," or choosing *not to compete*. Getting management's support for making that decision is often equally hard. No one likes to walk away from business, any business. The reason we sometimes stay when we should have "walked," however, is often because of fear.

What if there's not enough other business out there?

We hang on to "bad business" opportunities all the time because of this usually unstated fear: "If I walk away from this deal, in the hope that there are better opportunities out there, what happens if there aren't?" *Some salespeople actually resist assessing their current opportunities in real detail because they don't want to have to make this decision ...*

A "bad" opportunity can be one we can't win, but most sales reps want to believe in their ability to win any deal that comes their way. Bad opportunities can also be ones that will use up more resources than their potential return or worth — time, effort, expenses, travel, support, and so on. They're unprofitable for both the sales rep and the company. But walking away from a deal is like admitting cowardice. It just isn't done.

Fear is caused by the unknown.

The entire purpose for completing the territory and account plans is to make us face up to what we *do* know, what we *don't* know, and what we *need* to know about our selling marketplaces. Lack of knowledge creates selling fear, and fear generates *emotional* sales decisions, not good *business* decisions. The only antidote for this kind of fear is a comprehensive knowledge of the sales territory, combined with a practical business plan for success and a realistic assessment of the opportunity at hand. It's the only way to have the confidence that there are more than sufficient opportunities for "good" business — and that we can afford to walk away from the marginal ones.

FIGURE 6.14. SECOND RULE OF OPPORTUNITY MANAGEMENT

THE 2nd RULE OF OPPORTUNITY MANAGEMENT

"There is as much good business as there is bad business!"

Why are we focusing on walking away from business? Isn't that a negative approach? Shouldn't we focus instead on how to win? The truth is that if you're not prepared to make the decision to walk, you're not prepared to sell.

Unfortunately, it is not true that a great salesperson can win every deal. I've known ones who could close just about every deal, but that's not necessarily "winning" in the framework of building *profitable customer relationships*. Remember the axiom, "don't confuse the sell with the install," and where that gets us? What we want to develop are salespeople who can win every deal they *should* win!

Therefore, the Opportunity Assessment and Planning step involves gathering the initial information we need to do two things:

1. Decide to compete
2. Develop an Opportunity Plan to win.

To make this decision and begin to develop the Opportunity Plan, we need to get solid answers to ten important questions.

TEN ASSESSMENT AND PLANNING QUESTIONS

1. What was the customer's event or situation that created this opportunity?

I asked a prospect, "What was the event or situation that made you decide to look for sales training for your people?" The answer I received was, "Well, we want to make them more effective salespeople!"

"No," I said, "what happened in your company that caused someone to say, 'I think we need to invest in sales training'?" That creates very different answers that can tell us a lot about the viability of an opportunity.

What would your opinion of this opportunity be if the prospect answered, "Sales are down, and we think our people need more advanced skills to win against the competition"? There's a good solid need you can work with and justify the cost of your product.

What if the answer was, "Well, there's nothing really going on right now, but we're in our slow season and thought it might be a good time to do some skills development"? It's not necessarily a bad opportunity, but there's no critical need that's driving it. In other words, this deal could go away tomorrow for no good reason.

And what if the answer was, "Rather than getting into that, could you just give us a proposal?" The best case is that they see you and your products as a commodity; the worst case is that you're a victim of the "Three-Vendor Policy." In other words, they've already selected a vendor (not you), but the company's purchasing policy requires them to get three proposals.

Knowing the event or situation that generated the initial interest is a critical step in getting the "lay of the land."

2. What is the customer's perceived need?
(The business issue they are trying to solve)

How many times have we received a customer RFP (Request for Proposal) or a phone call that tells us exactly what the customer wants to buy? The prospect presents us with a "spec sheet" list—a list of *product needs*—and their only question for vendors is, "Can you provide this and at what price?"

I sold for the IBM Corporation in the 1970s. Although we sold computers, the standard sales approach was that we stayed away from talking about "computers." I was taught to focus on business issues and the *solutions* or results provided, even when the customer wanted to talk "product specs." Many times I said to a prospect, "Do you really care whether the reports you need (that will help you manage the business better) come out of a computer or the back of that chair? Aren't results are all that matter?"

If that didn't refocus the prospect back to business needs, I told a story that I had been told during IBM sales training when I asked, "How does it (the computer) work?" For me this story illustrated the real difference between selling product specifications and real business solutions:

> *Once upon a time up in the Yukon Territory, a grizzled old prospector wandered into a town, his cases filled with gold. Now, that prospector was a bit of a hermit and hadn't seen civilization for more than fifty years. In that town was a camping store with the latest technology in tents and sleeping bags and the like, and the old prospector was naturally drawn to it.*
>
> *The young salesman who helped the prospector couldn't believe his luck. In the process of showing him the newest "camping technologies," the prospector picked up a thermos bottle and asked, "What's this?"*
>
> *"Well," said the salesman, "you'll really like this. Imagine, in the winter when it's fifty-below outside, you pour your hot coffee in the thermos, and it keeps it hot all day!" The prospector was amazed at such a thing. But being on a roll and not knowing it's wise to quit selling when you've won the sale, the salesman continued, "And in the summer when it's so hot out, you can pour ice-cold stream water in the thermos, and it will keep it cold all day long!"*
>
> *The old prospector just scratched his head. "But how does it know?" he asked.*
>
> *The answer is, "Don't worry about it, it just does."*

I remember my frustration a few years later when I worked for another large computer manufacturer. Their philosophy at the time was that they sold computers: "Tell us what you need, and we'll give you a price." No one even wondered what the customer was going to do with it. No one even asked. The customer decided if he *needed* my product; I presented specifications and negotiated the price (and no one needs sales reps for that anymore).

Today we're interested in the *business need or situation* — the issue the customer is attempting to address — not the product feature shopping list. In fact, what we really want to know is why customers believe their "spec sheet" represents the best possible solution to their business issue driving the opportunity! There's something else to consider when presented with a spec sheet or RFP. Where did it come from and by whom was it influenced? It is interesting how often RFPs closely resemble the spec sheet or proposal of the vendor who got there first.

3. What is the customer's *vision* of the ideal solution?

When prospects tell us about the event that generated the opportunity and the business need they are trying to solve, a typical response is something like, "Great, now let me tell you how our 'Master Widget' can take care of that for you!" Rarely does anyone ask the customer what he or she thinks the ideal solution would be.

The importance of bringing out the customers' existing vision of the ideal solution will de discussed in much more detail in the section, *Vision* Selling, but suffice it to say that knowing how closely the customers' preconceived view of the solution is to the solution we offer is a critical assessment tool. The degree of *alignment* is a good early indicator of the relative ease or difficulty of the selling effort before us.

4. What are the specific results expected?

What are the tangible results the customer expects after the sale? Can we achieve them? How will they be measured? What if the prospect's expectations are unrealistic in our opinion?

A potential client once told me the "measurable" results the company expected to achieve with the pilot of a sales automation system after the first ninety days. These results would be used by corporate to assess whether the project would be continued. Everyone in the meeting, including the software vendor, nodded right along throughout the presentation. Later, I told them that based on my experience with similar companies, their expectations would be almost impossible to achieve. Actually the word I used was *doomed*. They were not amused.

Whether I could successfully "re-engineer" that client's expectations was an important factor in determining the success of our long-term relationship and whether I would be able to use this client as a reference to leverage new business with other customers.

5. Is the project or purchase funded?

Are funds currently available for this purchase? Are they already budgeted? If not, what will the process be to secure funding? How long will it take?

When funds are unbudgeted, but we're assured that it "shouldn't be a problem getting them approved," red flags should go up all around. Chances are—particularly in larger companies—that we may have *indirect competition* in addition to *direct* or product competitors. Indirect competitors are other organizations or departments within the company who are also seeking funding for their projects, often from the same "money tree" we're looking at. Not surprisingly, indirect competition can be far more difficult to overcome than direct competitors because we often have little knowledge of them and even less control.

6. What is the decision process?

This is really a two-part question. First, *who* is going to actually make the decision, *who* must approve it, and *who else* will be involved? Second, what is the *administrative* process for a decision for our particular type of product?

The first question, the *who*, is not just the task of collecting names but asking a key assessment question: "Do we have or can reasonably expect to get direct selling access to decision makers, approvers, and others who will significantly impact the buying decision?" The greater your access, the greater your potential to win!

I experienced a good example of the importance of knowing up front the second issue—timing and administrative process. A number of years ago, I had been working a large account for a fairly large sale of around $70,000. Everything had gone right, and I had the assurance of the vice president that the decision would be made before month's end and that I would be selected. So naturally I forecasted this deal at almost 100% to my manager.

That opportunity did not close for another six months. As promised, I did receive a call before month's end telling me that *I had won the business* and had been selected as the vendor. What I also learned was that company policy required capital purchases in excess of $50,000 to be approved by the Capital Appropriations Committee. The good news was that I was assured that approval would be "no problem"; the bad news was they only met quarterly, and their agenda was already full for the next meeting.

Although the sale finally did close, during the six months of waiting for approval, we had to deal with several attacks of the "FUDs" ("fears, uncertainties, and doubts") by the VP and a few last-minute direct and indirect competitive attacks. In short, making the sale required far more resources and time than I had ever anticipated because I neglected to fully investigate the decision-making process in that company.

7. What's driving the "driver"?

Who is really driving the purchase? What is this person's stake in the project or the purchase? What will the impact be on him or her personally? Will it be increased prestige or power, or the resolution of a problem that currently threatens his or her position or security? In short, the personal benefit to the driver is a pretty good indicator of how we should direct our sales presentations.

8. How is the product fit?

Given everything we've learned from answering all the previous questions, how close does the fit of our product to customer needs appear at this point? How competitive are we?

9. What leverage will winning this opportunity give us?

What other opportunities might be leveraged by winning this sale? We want to look at this question from all possible points of view and attempt to realistically identify and assess the answers. For example:

1. Continuing follow-on sales, upgrades, etc. (How much? Over what period of time?)
2. Ability to sell other products to the same buyers (What future opportunities will these same contacts likely be involved in?)
3. Other known or anticipated opportunities in this account
4. Opportunities in the parent company, subsidiaries, affiliates, or divisions
5. Leverage to sell to new companies in this industry or sales territory
6. Impact the install base of a competitor

10. What *critical business needs* are we going to focus on to create a competitive advantage with value products?

To answer this last and most important question, we have to *plan our attack*—that is, decide which of the nine "value products" will form the basis of our overall sales strategy. If we answered the first nine questions completely, then we should have a fairly reliable sense of what the customer is looking for and which ones they will respond to.

Which value products are our probable strengths in this specific opportunity? How does the prospect view these now? This is especially important if we have worked with the prospect, in the past. (Even if we are selling to a new prospect, we should ask ourselves what we believe his or her initial opinion may be of us.) What are the competitive "vulnerability targets"? What is our plan to develop and improve the value perception?

The following is a sample "STRATEGY MAPPING Opportunity Assessment and Planning Analysis" form that builds a simple and usable framework for evaluating a potential sale:

STRATEGY MAP OPPORTUNITY PLAN

KEY ACCOUNT: SUPERIOR INDUSTRIES
OPPORTUNITY TITLE: PROJECT A

Opportunity	Assessment
Prospect event or situation that created this opportunity	Superior realized they had a problem with _____ and it had the following impact on them: declining revenues that have adversely affected stock price. Chief Financial Officer is very upset; wants issue resolved ASAP!
Customer-perceived need	Superior believes they need to improve _____ by doing the following: (Example: purchasing X)
Customer vision of optimal solution and anticipated results	Superior's perception of the ideal solution is: The expected results are: (Attach technical requirements summary.)
Funding source budgeted? Available?	Funds from this purchase are already allocated in the amount of . . . .

Decision process and date	Decision date is by June 30. The following are the steps in the decision process and the individuals responsible:
"Driver" contact and personal motive	"John Smith" is driving this project. His issues and objectives are:
Proposed product solution	I plan to propose "Product 1" because ....
Revenue $$	Anticipated revenue is ....
Alignment with prospect needs and buy motive	

KEY OPPORTUNITY PLANNING

Strategic Value of this Opportunity

Potential Follow-on Sales Opportunities Leveraged by This Opportunity

Opportunity	Active Y/N	Products	$ Potential	Competitor
1. Add-on sales	N	Widget	$50,000	Floppo
2. ABC (Affiliate)	Y	Maxi Widget	$75,000	None

Opportunity Perceived-Value Analysis (Nine business needs)

Value ("We provide this account …. ")	Provided?	Perception
Product or Service for Resale		
Funding (sales, investment, terms, etc.)		
Operations (physical operation of the business)	X	3
Competitive Advantage — increase	X	3
Customer Satisfaction — increase	X	3
Information — uniquely available		
Expertise — not available internally		
Profits — increase		
Opportunity — increase sales opportunities		
	TOP 3 TOTAL	9

Opportunity Advantage/Vulnerability Position

Score	Position
11–15	High Competitive Advantage/Low Vulnerability to Competitive Intrusion
6–10 XX	Competitive Parity, No Perceived Advantage, Moderate Vulnerability
0–5	Competitive Disadvantage/High Vulnerability to Competitive Intrusion

Key Competitor Perceived-Value Analysis (Nine business needs)

Value ("They provide this account … .")	Provided?	Perception
Product or Service for Resale		
Funding (sales, investment, terms, etc.)		
Operations (physical operation of the business)		
Competitive Advantage — increase		
Customer Satisfaction — increase		
Information — uniquely available		
Expertise — not available internally		
Profits — increase	X	5
Opportunity — increase sales opportunities		
	TOP 3 TOTAL	5

Competitor Vulnerability Targets

Value	Strategy
Operations	Show that competitor has no plan to help in this area.
Competitive Advantage	Show how we have developed this for others.
Customer Satisfaction	Deliver report showing how we develop more satisfied customers than competitor.

Top Three "One-Point Plan"

Detail strategy to improve "Top 3" selected value perceptions by 1 point:

1. We can improve customer's perception of our ability to improve his operation by doing the following:
   A. Provide reference stories
   B. Customer visit

2. We can improve customer's perception of our ability to improve his competitive advantage by doing the following:

A. Provide technical summary data

B. Show superior new products currently under development

3. We can improve customer's perception of our ability to increase his satisfaction by doing the following:

A. Provide testimonials

THE CONTACT FOCUS

As every salesperson and manager knows, selling ultimately comes down to the one-on-one relationship of selling face-to-face. The Contact Focus naturally follows the completion of the Opportunity Assessment and Plan and the decision to compete.

FIGURE 6.15. THE CONTACT FOCUS

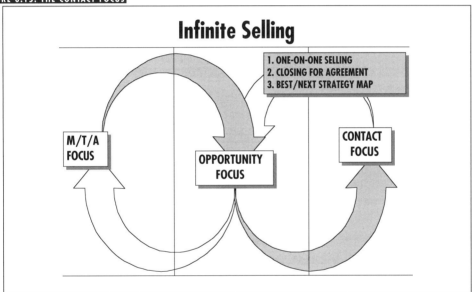

The Contact Focus begins by first *understanding buyer roles*, that is, more specifically determining the role each contact will play in the final decision of this specific sales opportunity, and how the contact fits within the real *decision power structure* (keeping in mind that the decision organization chart may not really mirror the corporate one). The second element of the Contact Focus is *closing through gaining contact agreement* — determining exactly what each contact must agree to in order to support us in the final decision and gaining that agreement through a new selling process called VISION SELLING.

BUYER ROLES — WHO'S ON FIRST?

Ask sales reps why "deals" fall apart all too often at the last minute and too often in opportunities that are forecasted at a high percentage of closing. Some of the most common answers are these:

- "Suddenly they were looking at a new competitor at the eleventh hour — one we didn't even know about!"

- "Our contact in the account said we were home free, but then the project got canceled (or delayed)."

- "They picked the competitor! I can't believe it! We clearly had a better solution (product, price). How could they make that decision?"

- "We answered the RFP (request for proposal) perfectly. We should have gotten it!"

- "Our contact said he was the only one we needed to talk to, and then somebody else made the final decision."

Fundamentally, any deal that falls apart at the last minute for reasons like these tells us that we didn't really know what was going on in the opportunity. In other words, there should have been no surprises; every possibility should have been anticipated and prepared for. The objective is to "control" the progression of the sales opportunity; something that is impossible if we lack information about what is really going on during the decision process. Once again, "it's what you don't know that kills you!"

Very rarely do deals just "fall apart." Someone, somewhere in the decision cycle made a decision to our detriment — to let the competition in the door or not to allocate funds, and so forth. The point is that a decision was made that we were not in a position to influence.

FIRST RULE OF BUYER RULES:
There is always more than one person in the buying process,
even if that's not what they would like to believe!

Human egos being what they are, salespeople run into "buyers" all the time who would have us believe either that they are the bottom-line decision maker or that the person who is the decision maker will rely entirely on their recommendation. Therefore, they may tell us that there is no need for us to talk to anyone else in the organization. In fact, it wouldn't even be appropriate because the senior executive (who shall remain nameless) has entrusted the decision entirely to them. What's more, that executive has supposedly specified that he or she has absolutely no interest in meeting with salespeople! Does this sound at all familiar?

Every deal has *the strong probability* of many people involved in the buying process who play one or more of several roles: **Decision Maker**, **Approver**, **Influencer**, **Observer**, or

Power Advocate. The keys are *identification* and *access*. To manage an opportunity and achieve the highest probability of success, we must (1) be able to identify who is in the buying process and his or her specific buyer role, and (2) gain effective access to each of them.

FIGURE 6.16. BUYER ROLES

OPPORTUNITY MANAGEMENT
Buyer Roles

Decision Maker - selects product

Approver - authorizes funds

Influencer - opinion required

Observer - opinion requested

Power Advocate - opens doors

Advocate - strong supporter

The Decision Makers.

The decision maker is the individual who will make the selection of the vendor and/or product. A decision maker may be the "selector" but is *not necessarily* the "buyer." He or she may need to have the "selection" *approved* by others and/or by committees. As such, a decision maker may be at any level of the corporation. The task of the salesperson, however, is to distinguish between a true decision maker and an *influencer* or recommender.

As a rule of thumb, a decision maker is someone who has been assigned (or has it in his or her direct power) to make a final selection, even if that decision requires another level of approval. Someone whose task is to select three finalists, do an analysis, or collect information is not a decision maker.

The Approvers.

An approver is the person or persons who, in one form or another, *sign the contract*. Approvers may be insulated from the selling process; that is, they may not participate directly in the vendor/product evaluation and selection process. Generally, they plan to rely on assigned decision makers.

Two issues need to be examined closely in sales situations where we identify approvers:

1. *How real is the deal?* Approvers, usually senior executives, often assign people to evaluate the *potential* of a purchase or of changing vendors, or just investigate new products and pricing. Naturally few "evaluators" want to tell a salesperson that they are literally "just looking" if they want the vendor's attention. Access to the approver is a critical tool if we are to fully qualify the sale.

2. *Top-down selling, or calling directly on an approver, could be a waste of time.* A common axiom of selling is "Call at the top." For example, a company whose salespeople were instructed to sell directly to CEOs of large corporations were successful at gaining access at this level. They consistently found their sales message well received, but despite the executive's apparent interest and enthusiasm, few sales actually resulted. What went wrong?

   Smart senior executives, especially in larger corporations, have taken "dancing lessons"; that is, they have learned *not to step on the toes of people they have hired or assigned to be "decision makers."* As interested as a top executive may be in our sales message, few will cut out their own people by making decisions without them. It's the surest way to develop personnel problems by implying a lack of trust in their ability to do the job for which they were hired. For this same reason, many resist even *recommending* that their decision makers see a vendor who has called directly on them in order to avoid the appearance of having a bias.

We know that we need access to approvers to assess the real viability of the opportunity and to have the best odds of closing the deal. The question is how?

Rather than attempting to gain access on our own, the solution is to be "taken to power" by a decision maker. To accomplish this, however, the decision maker must perceive a direct personal value. Why would a decision maker want a vendor to meet with the approver? The answer lies in value products and the decision maker's perceptions.

The *value products* (expertise, competitive advantage, profit, funding, and so on) represent the unique added-value we bring to the sale. When a decision maker perceives that value as an important benefit that will improve the success of the company *and bring him or her personal benefit* ("what's driving the driver?"), then the door magically opens to the executive or approver level. In effect, the decision maker has an opportunity to demonstrate that he or she is providing added value to the company *through us*!

SECOND RULE OF BUYER ROLES:
Access is everything!

The lesson here is that the access we want in a sales opportunity is *given* to us by our contacts, whatever their buyer role or level in the company. Contacts who perceive value themselves — and the potential value to others in the decision-making process — will open the doors of access for us.

The Influencers.

An influencer is someone who is *specifically assigned the task* of providing input, data, or a recommendation to and by the decision maker; that is, *his or her recommendation is required by the decision maker!* Influencers do, in fact, play an important role in the overall decision cycle and must be "sold" as firmly as the decision maker.

Just as decision makers are important for providing access to approvers, influencers can provide access to decision makers. What we need to avoid, however, are the influencers who only introduce us to other influencers, or worse, people beneath them in the decision process, the *observers*. Salespeople can get lost in the M.A.Z.E. of multiple influencers and observers, each of whom is eager to collect information and data and provide his or her recommendations but has little or no real power.

The Observers.

Observers are people who involve themselves in the buying process (often using up our resources with questions, requests for information or demonstrations, etc.) but who have not been specifically asked to do so by the decision maker. As a rule of thumb, *the observer's opinion (not recommendation) has been requested (not required) by an influencer (not a decision maker).*

Frequently, observers may be associates or departmental coworkers of an influencer who has brought them into the loop. In other words, an *observer is an influencer to an influencer.* Observers will offer an opinion, but it rarely plays a significant role in the actual buying process because it is so low in the overall power structure. This doesn't mean they can be ignored, but the resources we are willing to expend to "sell" observers should certainly be far less than for the other buyer roles.

As a side note, observers — and to some extent lower-level influencers — like to take the "safe" approach. Rather than making positive recommendations or recommending a specific purchase, it is easier (and much safer) to point out the negatives or possible downside risks. Few want to be remembered as a positive recommender if a product or vendor fails to perform or achieve the expected results. (It's easier to say "Well, I warned you!")

Even assuming we develop access to each of the key players in the buying process, the problem remains that most of us can't *live* at our prospect's location. Even if we spend as much time there as possible, we are still not privy to many of the internal conversations, evaluations, and meetings that will have much to do with our success. What we *really* need is someone who is "plugged in" to the entire decision process, who can tell us what's going on, and who is actively looking out for our interests.

The Power Advocate.

If there is one fundamental question that should be asked in determining whether or not a sales opportunity will or can be won, it is "Do we have a *power advocate?*" Why?

THIRD RULE OF BUYER ROLES:
If you don't have a power advocate,
chances are you're not going to close the sale!

There are two kinds of advocates, and it's important to distinguish between the two: the advocate and the power advocate.

An *advocate* is someone in the customer's organization who fully supports our sales effort. He or she firmly believes that the choice of our product or service is the best possible choice. We can't have too many advocates; every approver, decision maker, influencer, and observer should be one. There is no guarantee, however, that an advocate is in a position to actually do much of anything to help us in the sales effort.

In fact, it's easy to fall into an *advocate trap*. Every sales rep likes to call on someone who is firmly in his or her camp. The trap is sprung when we neglect calling on others in the cycle because of this relationship or we end up waiting and waiting for our advocate to help us gain access, only to find out too late that he or she really can't.

The *power advocate* is also a strong supporter with one fundamental difference. He or she has *personal power* and can actively work to influence the decision on our behalf as our inside salesperson *by providing access to decision makers, key influencers, and approvers.*

Criterion for the power advocate: Again, the most important criterion for us and task for the power advocate is whether this person can directly (and willingly) provide us access to higher levels and/or key players *with his or her personal recommendation.*

FIGURE 6.17. CRITERIA FOR THE POWER ADVOCATE

OPPORTUNITY MANAGEMENT

POWER ADVOCATE

Must be willing to ...

1. Be the Inside Salesperson
2. Define Players, Roles, & Path
3. Provide Access to Power
4. Take Personal Risk
5. Confront Competition
6. Direct to New Opportunities

"UNRECOGNIZED PROPHETS"

Critical GO/NO GO Decision Point!

As shown in Figure 6.17, we have a number of specific expectations and criteria to qualify a power advocate. For starters, this person must become our inside salesperson and be willing to take an active role in helping us work the buying process successfully and quickly. The power advocate is willing to publicly put him or herself on the line for us because he or she perceives a personal value in our successfully winning the sale.

Second only to providing access, however, is the power advocate's ability to provide us with the following inside information and assistance:

1. Us versus the competition. What are the competition's strengths and weaknesses *in the eyes of the prospect*? The power advocate can help us do a value analysis of the competition and help identify *vulnerability targets*.
2. Who is really for us, and who is really against us? Why?
3. Who are the advocates and power advocates for the competition? (Yes, they have them, too!)
4. Provide a warning of "hidden" competition or last-minute competitive intrusion and actively work to defuse it on our behalf.
5. Provide continuous viability assessment, such as forewarning when objectives may be changing, loss of funding, or of potential delays. The power advocate also gives us an accurate assessment of our competitive position as the leader, contender, or also-ran.
6. Provide continuing evaluations of customer satisfaction or post-sale issues.
7. Direct us to additional follow-on sales opportunities.

Can you make a sale without a power advocate? Of course, with luck. However, the power advocate smoothes the way and speeds the overall process *and dramatically reduces the risk of last-minute fallout.* Consider also that selling against a competitor's power advocate without one of our own (preferably more powerful than theirs!) significantly reduces the probability of the sale.

BUILDING A STRATEGY MAP
THROUGH THE BUYING PROCESS

Once all the players in the buying process have been identified and their roles clearly defined as decision makers, approvers, influencers, observers, or power advocates, the task of the salesperson is to develop a STRATEGY MAP or plan to chart the most efficient selling path of BEST/NEXT strategies and tactics.

The first part of a STRATEGY MAP is the BEST/NEXT Sequence and Access:

1. Determine whom we need to call on, in what sequence, and who can provide access to whom.
2. Identify probable value products that will help us gain access.

3. Determine individual sales strategies: "How are we going to achieve each contact's agreement to support us in the final decision?"

The following is a sample "Opportunity Contact Analysis" for planning this step in the sales process:

OPPORTUNITY CONTACT ANALYSIS (SAMPLE)

In the "Opportunity Contact Analysis," the salesperson identifies each of the known contacts who will play a role in the decision-making process for this specific opportunity. On this form we list each contact's name and title and indicate whether or not we have access to that individual. In other words, has the salesperson met this contact, and/or can he or she easily call on this person as needed throughout the sales cycle?

In the "Support" column, we indicate if the contact currently *supports (S)* the choice of our product or service in this opportunity, is *open (O)* to our product or service with no currently known vendor preference, or is *against (A)* or in opposition to choosing us or our product. If the contact is against, it is likely that he or she is a supporter of another vendor.

Finally, in the "Buyer Role" column, we indicate the role that each contact plays in this decision as a decision maker, influencer, approver, observer, advocate, or power advocate.

Contact	Title	Access	Support	Buyer Role
1. Bob Jones	Sales Manager	Yes	S	Power advocate/Influencer
2. Sheila Smith	CEO	No	O	Approver
3. Terry Robertson	VP, Sales and Marketing	Yes	O	Decision maker
4. Barry Cole	MIS Manager	Yes	A	Influencer
5. Anne Sherman	Operations	Yes	S	Advocate/Observer

Support: S = Support, O = Open, A = Against

Role: Decision maker, Influencer, Approver, Observer, Advocate, Power advocate

Contact Perceived-Value Analysis
(complete for each contact in buyer roles)

NAME: Bob Jones, Sales Manager, Power Advocate

Value ("We provide this account .... ")	Provided?	Perception
Product or Service for Resale		
Funding (sales, investment, terms, etc.)		
Operations (physical operation of the business)	X	4
Competitive Advantage — increase	X	4
Customer Satisfaction — increase		
Information — uniquely available		
Expertise — not available internally	X	5
Profits — increase		
Opportunity — increase sales opportunities		
	TOP 3 TOTAL	13

Advantage/Vulnerability Position

Score	Position
11 – 15 XX	High Competitive Advantage/Low Vulnerability to Competitive Intrusion
6 – 10	Competitive Parity, No Perceived Advantage, Moderate Vulnerability
0 – 5	Competitive Disadvantage/High Vulnerability to Competitive Intrusion

VISION SELLING—THE SALES CALL

VISION SELLING is a unique, *consultative* sales call methodology for identifying contact needs, goals, and issues; and *developing* them with the prospect to a *solution vision* that utilizes our product or service. At the same time it creates a coaching methodology for planning and assessing sales call effectiveness.

VISION SELLING is based on a five-step process which, like INFINITE SELLING, uses the model of the infinity loop.

FIGURE 6.18. VISION SELLING

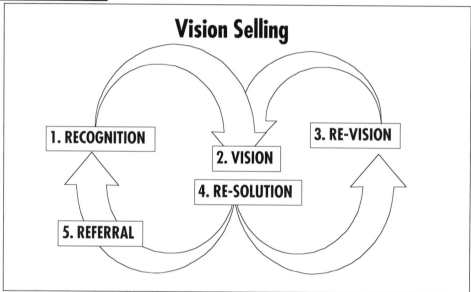

STEP 1: RECOGNITION

The one-on-one process of VISION SELLING begins with the Recognition Step. As in the following example, we ask questions that determine specifically what is the contact's personal *recognition* of the driving business issues and potential benefits that will be attained by making this purchase. What is the potential benefit to both the company and the contact?

> "Bob, before we talk about the product we offer, I'd like to get your perspective on what brought about your company's interest in buying (widgets). What is really driving this effort? Can you tell me more about what you see as the specific business issues driving this purchase and what you see as the most significant potential benefits to the company?"
>
> "How does (or will) this impact you?"

The purpose of this first step is to learn what this contact believes are the driving business issues behind the opportunity and what the potential impact is on him or her. The step is critical because people make buying decisions based on their perceptions of business and personal needs and benefits, which may not necessarily be the same as those of other contacts or as the company's stated goals.

Few salespeople take the time or make the effort to ask this kind of question, but doing so forms a solid base for the remainder of the sales call by telling the contact that we are interested in his or her perspective and opinion. Most salespeople instead launch immediately into a series of "qualifying" or "probing for information" questions. The message to the prospect, of course, is that the sales rep is only there to make a sale, not to help the customer find the best possible business solution.

As we learn about driving business issues, we should begin thinking about how these map to the *value products* we provide. For example, in addition to the physical product we sell, will our *expertise* play a role in the final solution? If the customer is looking for a more reliable or higher quality product, does that map to *customer satisfaction* or perhaps *competitive advantage*?

Equally important is the second question, "How does this (that is, not resolving the business issue or problem) impact you?" No two contacts will be affected in the same way, and most will be surprised we asked!

STEP 2: VISION

The Vision Step is without question *the most difficult task in selling* for a salesperson. It's the step that many cannot bring themselves to actually do. Probably as a result of its difficulty, it is consequently one of the most powerful tactics in selling. In the Vision Step we ask the contact a single question:

"Bob, what do you see as the ideal solution?"

One sentence. Why so difficult? Why so powerful? Why so necessary?

It is so very difficult because the answer to the Vision question might not be one we want to hear. It may be 180 degrees away from our product or service, based on features and capabilities we cannot offer. It may even be a specific competitor's product! The salesperson may feel "blown out of the water" before he or she even starts! Consider this:

I can't change your mind if I don't know what you think!

By not asking the Vision question, we have no idea how to focus our sales presentation most effectively. Even more important, as we said earlier, *it's what you don't know that kills you!* Preconceived ideas won't necessarily go away if we make a great sales presentation, especially if we don't know what they are. A contact who appears to be in agreement with us early on may late in the sales process surface his or her issues and different solution *visions* — especially when we are in no position to counter them.

We derive some other very solid benefits by asking this question, as well. First, it provides a *base* for our selling strategy with this contact; we know where we stand going in. Second, it changes the contact's perception of us from salesperson to consultant. As one contact said, "No salesperson has ever asked me what I thought the best solution was!"

Why is the consultant perception so important? Because people listen with an *open mind* to people they perceive as educators and consultants. People's minds are at least partially closed to salespeople whom they fear will "convince" them or pressure them to do something they really don't want to do. What is *your* reaction to a retail store salesperson who says, "May I help you?" The response, "No thanks, just looking" really means, "If I can't find what I want I'll call you, but I don't want you to pressure me into a purchase."

If we are going to sell effectively, we need contacts who will listen to us with an open mind, opened by the Vision question.

STEP 3: RE-VISION

Re-Vision is the process of working with the contact to *re-engineer the vision* or build a new or enhanced vision of an ideal solution based upon the products or services we offer. We use value products as the tool to begin this process.

The process of Re-Vision starts with a statement by the salesperson, as simple as:

> *"Thank you, Bob. I appreciate getting your perspectives. May I make some suggestions (or recommendations) that I believe might help you achieve even better results?"*

Notice that nowhere did we say or even suggest that the contact's vision is wrong, misinformed, or shortsighted. Even a phrase such as *suggestions which you* should *consider* can immediately develop resistance. What we *have* done is ask permission to "enhance" the contact's vision. Few people will deny us this opportunity.

The temptation is to leap into an immediate product presentation. But to maintain the contact's open-mindedness, first we need to *refocus the contact on value products,* as in the following conversation:

> *"Bob, from what you've told me so far about your issues and goals, it seems to me that in addition to the specific issues that need to be addressed, there are*

really three major business objectives—or what I call 'critical business needs'—that you're trying to address. Specifically, you are looking for a product or service that will first improve the effectiveness and lower the costs of operations; second, at the same time improve customer satisfaction; and third, improve the bottom-line profit picture. Is that an accurate assessment?"

Assuming a "yes" answer, we can follow with:

"Many of our customers have those same objectives and, like you, have investigated a number of possible solutions. What they found was that our (approach, products, services, capabilities) provided them a higher return on their investment than the other options, and here is why. ..."

What really is happening here? We first focused the contact's attention *away from* product specifications and vendor comparisons *toward* bottom-line business results. Now we can present product specifics within the framework of how each will help achieve the global business objectives identified.

"For example, Bob, I strongly recommend our A-12 Model Widget for these reasons. ..."

Finally, of course, we test or end the Re-Vision step with some variation of the great qualifying and pre-closing questions:

"Do you agree, Bob, that this sounds like an optimal solution?"

"If we can prove (this) to your satisfaction, will I have your support when the final decision is made?"

STEP 4: RE-SOLUTION — THE PROOF STEP

As the name of this step suggests, its purpose is to prove our new or re-engineered solution that may have been very different from the one the contact initially had in mind. In so doing we will bring the sales process with this contact to resolution, that is, assuring his or her support.

What is the most expedient and effective way to go about proving our capabilities to the contact? In some companies the immediate answer might be, "Let's do a demo!" or build a prototype or do an existing customer visit or any number of resource-intensive choices.

Proof should initially be given by using the fewest resources necessary to meet the customer's requirement for proof!

In other words, don't expend more time and resources than you must in order to prove your points, or you risk opening Pandora's Box with proof sources that generate new issues or questions.

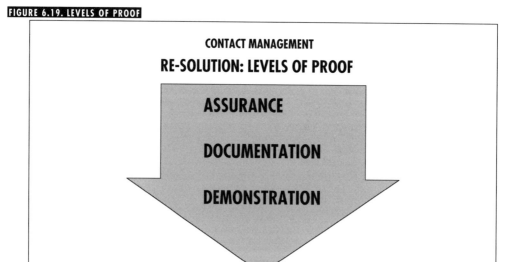

FIGURE 6.19. LEVELS OF PROOF

CONTACT MANAGEMENT
RE-SOLUTION: LEVELS OF PROOF

ASSURANCE

DOCUMENTATION

DEMONSTRATION

RESOURCES EXPENDED

So what is the best way to prove we can fulfill the *Re-Vision* we created with the contact? The answer is that there are three levels of logical proof, each requiring more resources (and risk), which should be used *in sequence*: *assurance, documentation,* and *demonstration*.

First Level of Proof: Assurance.

Assurance is exactly what it sounds like: assuring the contact verbally that we can in fact do what we said we could. Typically, assurance requires a detailed explanation on the part of the salesperson (or a technical consultant brought in for this purpose) of exactly how we will accomplish this. It requires a bit more effort than telling the contact "No problem!" Stronger assurance may be provided through senior management visits or by telephone conversations with existing customers who are willing to *assure* the prospect of your capabilities.

It has always surprised me how often *assurance* is an acceptable and adequate form of proof, requiring no further efforts. It is, however, directly related to the extent to which the contact regards us as consultants who are knowledgeable about the contact's business and goals.

Second Level of Proof: Documentation.

When assurance alone is inadequate, we move to the second level of proof—tangible *documentation*. Documentation may take many different forms, usually written. These include product specification sheets or more detailed product documents, written customer testimonials and references, benchmark performance data, industry reports, and so forth.

Third Level of Proof: Demonstration.

The final level of proof, *demonstration*, requires the most resources expended and creates the highest degree of risk because it opens the product up in its entirety to view by the customer — and may create more concerns and problems than it resolves. The demonstration must be highly controlled and directed at pre-agreed specific product functions.

Demonstration is the last resort of the proof process.

It is probably worthwhile to comment on the purpose and use of the product demo. Some salespeople use the demo as a "selling tool" ("Why don't I come out and give you a demo?") that they offer or because a prospect asks for one early in the sales cycle. The idea is to show the product to gain prospect interest in a "throw it against the wall and see what sticks" scenario. In point of fact, however, the *demonstration is properly a closing tool*, not a selling one. Its purpose is to *prove* our capabilities to meet a customer's understood needs and our ability to provide value products!

STEP 5: REFERRAL

VISION SELLING is based on the infinity symbol because, like INFINITE SELLING, there needs to be more to "closing" the contact for support on a given opportunity. The end result should not only be contact agreement but also a willingness to *refer* us.

Referral may be a willingness to provide *access* in the buying cycle. It may also be direct *referrals* to other opportunities or agreement to be a *reference* to other companies.

STRATEGY MAP
BEST/NEXT SEQUENCE OF SALES TACTICS

SEQUENCE:	First tactic, 2/1/96
CONTACT:	John Smith
TITLE:	Manufacturing Manager
BUYER ROLE:	Influencer
1. RECOGNITION	Cannot meet customer service goals because of poor forecasting; he is getting pressure to fix the problem.
2. VISION	Problem is with sales. They should be made to forecast more accurately by management.
3. RE-VISION	Sales automation would enable him to constantly monitor opportunity progress, not just rely on percentage closing estimates.
4. RE-SOLUTION	Have John speak to Ed Jones, at ABC Co., who will tell him how they did this and the excellent customer service results.
BEST/NEXT TACTIC	Schedule phone call with Ed Jones for next week and confirm with Smith.

SEQUENCE:	Second tactic, 3/1/96
CONTACT:	Lorraine DePolo
TITLE:	VP, Sales
BUYER ROLE:	Decision maker, power advocate
1. RECOGNITION	Sales and profits are down, missing goals, frustrated because she can't get accurate, timely rolled-up sales pipeline info.
2. VISION	SFA is the solution, but only if her sales managers agree.
3. RE-VISION	We provide the best SFA solution for her reps and sales managers because ….
4. RE-SOLUTION	Meet with each of the sales managers, review concerns, do proposal, and present findings/recommendations to her.
BEST/NEXT TACTIC	Schedule meetings with sales managers, Bob Weeks, Robert Hamm, and Kerri Wallace-Reilly.

SEQUENCE:	Third tactic, 3/10/96
CONTACT:	Kerri Wallace-Reilly
TITLE:	Sales Manager
BUYER ROLE:	Influencer
1. RECOGNITION	Does not see why there is a problem. Management overreacting to a temporary slump in sales.
2. VISION	Best solution is to tighten up management of the reps — get them making more calls — or make some changes!
3. RE-VISION	Present the advantages of sales progress management over activity tracking with SFA to get maximum sales results.
4. RE-SOLUTION	Deliver "whitepaper" report on sales progress management.
BEST/NEXT TACTIC	Deliver whitepaper and set up follow-up meeting to discuss and review SFA capabilities.

The illustration above shows a completed sample STRATEGY MAP that ties together all the VISION SELLING concepts of STRATEGY MAPPING with BEST/NEXT strategies and tactics. (Note: A blank copy of this form is included in Chapter 8, "The Sales Manager's Survival Kit.")

For each contact, we identify the buying role in this opportunity, his or her *recognition* of the current issue and ideal *vision* of the solution, the *re-vision* we plan to create, and the *re-solution*, or how we plan to prove it.

Additionally, we have added the tactical element of BEST/NEXT. For each contact, what is our BEST/NEXT planned action *for that individual* to move closer to achieving his or her agreement for support?

Finally, each BEST/NEXT tactic is *sequenced* in the order (or by target date) we plan to execute it. The result then becomes a well-organized strategic and tactical "Action Plan" of the shortest route to the close — a plan that is continuously updated.

SUMMARY: INFINITE SELLING — COMPLETING THE LOOP

After completing the Contact focus — that is, we have received sufficient "Agreements for Support" to enable us to close — the INFINITE SELLING loop returns to the Opportunity Focus for final closing of the opportunity.

FIGURE 6.20. COMPLETING THE INFINITE SELLING LOOP

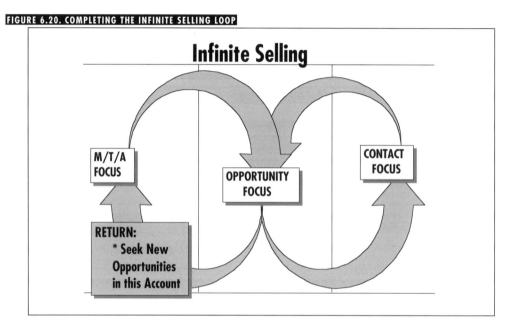

Typically, at this focus we deliver the *proposal* (which has already been agreed to de facto), negotiate contracts and/or terms, take the finalized order, deliver/install, and assure overall customer satisfaction.

Finally, we progress or return to where we began, the *Market/Territory/Account focus*. The point of logically returning here is that we now need to seek new business, which will generate new opportunities — perhaps in the market at large, perhaps in the account we just sold to. In any case, the current opportunity that we just successfully closed, delivered, and assured a satisfied customer becomes the *propulsion* we need to find and win new deals.

SUPPORTING STRATEGY MAPPING IN SALES AUTOMATION

Supporting the elements of the STRATEGY MAPPING methodology generally requires a sales force automation software package, which provides three data views or orientations and which includes the communications capabilities to share information across the sales enterprise. The following outlines the requirements of a *basic* system:

1. Account Orientation. User definable data fields containing at a minimum basic account information (company name, address, industry data, SIC codes, etc.). *All* existing contacts, opportunities, and activity data are linked to the account record.

2. **Opportunity Orientation.** Data are kept on specific sales opportunities, such as opportunity name, revenue potential, anticipated close date, product/service solution, etc. Contacts can be directly linked to the opportunity as well as activities and To-Do's. In other words, an opportunity may be viewed as a subset of the total account data in the system.

3. **Contact Orientation.** Basic contact manager data are kept to include name, specific address and telephone, and linked activities, as well as To-Do's.

The following data fields should be added to the appropriate data tables or files to provide basic support for STRATEGY MAPPING.

Account Table

Field Name	Description
Industry	Primary industry and/or SIC
Market*	Typical customer profile
Position	Growing/declining/stable
Revenues	Annual sales
Affiliates*	Parent company/subsidiaries/affiliates/divisions
Products*	Major products and services
Short Term*	Short-term goals and objectives
Obstacles*	Anticipated obstacles/competition

(*Indicates this field may require linking to "notes" or comment fields because of large blocks of text that may need to be entered.)

Opportunity Table

Field Name	Description
Event	Event/situation that created opportunity
Need	Business issues to be solved
Vision	Vision of ideal solution/vendor
Results*	Customer's expectations — long- and short-term results
Funding	Availability and source
Decision*	General description of decision process
Fit*	Strengths/weaknesses of product fit
Compete*	Key competitors' strengths and weaknesses
Value (3)	Selection of value products for sales strategy
OppScore	Gross value perception score
Vulnerable	Selection of competitor vulnerability targets

(*Indicates this field may require linking to "notes" or comment fields because of large blocks of text that may need to be entered.)

Contact Table

Field Name	Description
Buyer Role	Buyer role of contact in current opportunity
Access	Do we have access to this contact? Yes/No
Support	Supporter/Open/Against
Recognition*	Business issues to be solved and their impact
Vision*	Contact's vision of ideal solution/vendor
Re-Vision*	Proposed product/service solution
Re-Solution*	Proof sources
Value (3)	Selection of value products for sales strategy
ValScore	Gross value perception score

(*Indicates this field may require linking to "notes" or comment fields because of large blocks of text that may need to be entered.)

Activity and To-Do Tables

Field Name	Description
Best/Next*	BEST/NEXT activity planned (contact linked/date)
Milestone	Identifies the current milestone process step

(*Indicates this field may require linking to "notes" or comment fields because of large blocks of text that may need to be entered.)

CHAPTER 7

WINNING THE GAME OF SALES MANAGEMENT IN NINE INNINGS

WARM-UPS — THE CONFESSIONS OF A LITTLE LEAGUE MANAGER

We are managing salespeople into a new generation of selling — a generation requiring new sales methodologies augmented by new technologies. Terms such as *added-value* and *profitability* are gaining new meaning and new importance. A salesperson can no longer head out into the territory without a firm strategy backed by solid information.

As much as the realm of sales is changing, we have seen that managing is changing as well. The manager is becoming a coach, a mentor, an active participant in the competitive advantage equation. The old techniques of managing just won't work anymore. As much as salespeople need new selling and planning models, sales managers need new models for coaching, mentoring, and motivating, especially to maximize the potential of sales automation.

The biggest challenge for managers, and perhaps the most difficult, is managing change. Change is difficult for anyone at anytime, but it becomes especially so for salespeople who are asked to change how they work and how they sell, when they may not even perceive change is needed.

As I developed my thoughts about what the new management role should be and which skills today's managers really needed, I found myself continually going back to a series of both good and bad experiences that taught me most of what I really believe about effective management. Surprisingly, these events had little to do with selling, but everything to do with effectively managing salespeople.

Rather than pretend that I learned all this directly from years of sales management, I decided to tell "the truth" and let the reader learn the same way I did. These are the confessions of a Little League manager.

This is how one sales manager learned a lot more about sales management (at least the parts that worked) from a group of children than he ever did in business. Someone once said that child psychology works better on adults than it does on children. Maybe that's true; all I know is that almost everything I know about sales management *that worked* I learned from a nine-year-old. The names have been changed to protect me from coaches and parents.

THE FIRST SEASON

The day I was first promoted to sales manager I felt as though I had finally made it to the big time; my career was on its way; fame, glory, and more promotions were ahead. Life was getting easy. *What fools we mortals be.*

I had been a fairly good sales rep with all the usual ups and downs — fortunately with more ups than downs — and I thought I had some real experience to offer the salespeople in my new unit. Most important, I was going to be the kind of manager I had always wanted to have myself. I had a vision that my salespeople would come to me (their leader and font of all wisdom) to ask my counsel, to be coached on tactics and strategies. They would leave motivated, and together we would forge ahead to new heights of sales glory.

I was confident. I had just returned from *advanced* sales management training where I had been taught the *secrets* of sales motivation and coaching! In retrospect, it might have been better if I had been committed to an institution for the "managerially insane."

I probably don't need to describe what that first year of sales management was like. It was a grounding in reality. I was frustrated and found myself spending most of my time tracking activity, managing the office, and rolling up information for top management. Perhaps what saved me was that I became a sales manager and a Little League coach the same year.

Because I was clearly insane — and frustrated beyond belief at the time — may explain why I took up coaching kids' baseball. I did it because Casey, my then eight-year-old son, told me that he really wanted me to be the coach of his team! In other words, when the Cardinals needed a coach, Casey offered his dad. I've since observed that only eight-year-olds actually *want* Dad to be their coach, a desire that reverses itself dramatically just about the time Dad actually *wants* to be a coach.

Actually, I wasn't quite as confident about coaching baseball players as coaching salespeople, possibly because what I know about baseball is about as much as I know about differential calculus (which I think is a kind of high-tech car transmission or something). My brief personal career as a Little League player had been less than stellar because I couldn't hit, catch, or throw — a limitation on most teams. At least I'd done better as a sales rep!

So I joined the coaching ranks of the Merrimack, New Hampshire, Youth Association. On the first day of practice, I was assured by Walter, the Cardinal's manager (I was his assistant), that all I had to do was read the *Official Rule Book* and 230 pages of *U Can Coach Youth Baseball*, and I would do just fine. Lies, all lies!

I now have a rule in life. I have a hard time believing anyone named Walter. I know it's not fair, but I was scarred by the experience. I haven't seen Walter for fifteen years. More precisely, I haven't seen Walter since that first practice when he gave me my reading materials. Walt wasn't looking for an assistant; he was looking for a replacement. Ten minutes before our first game, "Mrs. Walt" drove up to the field, dropped off the equipment, and told me that Walter would be "a little late." She meant for the whole season.

So the first season wasn't perfect. The kids didn't know that I was lost, and when it was all over, Casey was still willing to acknowledge me as his father—privately if not publicly. I got the sympathy vote from most of the parents, and we won one game. Maybe part of the problem that year was that I never could quite figure out the left field and right field issue. (If you're standing on home plate looking out, is right field the one on the right or the left? You laugh, but are you sure?)

So, what made me believe I could coach baseball? I believed that all my training in sales motivation and coaching would work miracles with kids. After all, I had been trained in *advanced* managerial skills for coaching *adults* in the serious and sophisticated world of business, and these were just children in a kids' game! Piece of cake! I would get them fired up, get those competitive juices flowing, and develop a burning will to win. Combined with a few volunteer parents who could actually teach them how to play, we'd do just fine! I still think the concept was excellent—stupid, but excellent.

I must now tell you the two things I learned that first year as a new sales manager and as a new Little League coach. *First, traditional management skills don't work especially well with kids. Second, traditional management skills don't work much better with salespeople.* Before I incur the wrath of coaches and management trainers everywhere, I will concede that perhaps somewhere in a land far, far away with sales managers far better than I. … Well, you get the idea.

Why didn't my new management skills work with my salespeople? To begin with, the salespeople were far more interested in being left alone than in being motivated or coached. Somehow I'd forgotten that when I was a rep, I felt exactly the same way: "I haven't got time for this; I'm busy selling!!" Not only didn't *they* have the time for coaching and motivation, I found out that neither did I, with all the tracking and reporting I was supposed to be doing. All the *quality time* that was supposed to be spent by the manager helping and directing the salespeople was really spent the other way around—the salesperson *educating* the manager on what's new.

I wanted to be a leader; I found out I was a policeman. Mostly I made sure the sales reps were making enough calls and following up those leads, and I was giving them congratulations when they won and giving them hell when they lost. My weekly training and motivation sales meetings too quickly became "We better sell something this week, people!" sessions. Strangely enough, that also described my pregame speeches to my baseball players as we progressed through the season.

Despite rough starts in both areas, for the next fifteen years I managed both a sales force and a Little League team, and it was baseball that taught me how to really manage selling, not the other way around. So, inning by inning, here's what I learned.

FIGURE 7.1. THE GAME OF MANAGEMENT

NINE INNINGS OF SALES MANAGEMENT

1st Inning: THE 4 BASE-ICS:
　　　　　　Equipment, Skill, Strategy, Team
2nd Inning: THE GAME PLAN
3rd Inning: WHO WINS THE GAME?
4th Inning: PLAY THE BENCH
5th Inning: LOVE THOSE PRACTICES
6th Inning: PLAY BY THE RULES
7th Inning: MOTIVATION
8th Inning: PULLING THE PITCHER
9th Inning: THE DRAFT — Picking Winners

FIRST INNING: THE FOUR BASE-ICS TO THE CHAMPIONSHIP

You too can have a championship Little League team or top sales unit in just four easy steps (well OK, maybe not *that* easy), and here they are:

FIRST BASE: GET THE BEST EQUIPMENT!

Nine-year-old Joey's father, known to one and all as "Big Joe," was All-State in his high school baseball career, and Joey was going to follow in his footsteps despite not quite having Dad's talent. At the first game, Joey showed up with his dad's personal championship glove and home-run hitting bat. This was the fine equipment that had made Dad a star, and he had passed it down to Joey. But things have changed since "Big Joe" was in high school.

Yes, even youth baseball has gone high-tech. Gloves are bigger, wider, with deeper pockets, and catching a hit or a thrown ball has become easier. Aluminum bats replaced wood simply because they hit farther. The newest baseball bats are made of molded carbon-graphite, which drives a ball even farther. The point is that what was good enough for Dad may not be good enough for Joey, and understanding that may be difficult for both of them. Joey can't be competitive with out-of-date equipment, no matter how much talent he has. In our first two games, kids with less natural talent but with better equipment than Joey simply outplayed him. "Big Joe" took it even harder than Joey.

The *equipment* of selling has also changed. As we know, notebook computers are running sales automation software; there are on-line marketing encyclopedias, remote fax technology, product configurators and more with cellular phones and wireless data communications, and territory mapping and analysis software. All these are tools that can realistically improve sales effectiveness. In other words, automated salespeople have the potential to outsell their nonautomated (and perhaps even more talented) competitors.

One problem is that sales managers can be a lot like Joe's dad. We know what worked for us as sales reps, and we are most comfortable managing salespeople to work the same way we did. It's especially hard because before today's information and technology explosion, the equipment of selling had not really changed all that much in the last hundred years. So salesperson Joe and his sales manager "Dad" may both find it difficult to adjust to this change and may delay *upgrading their equipment* until it's too late. As in baseball, the best equipment is no guarantee of winning, but among competitors, when all other things are equal, the best equipment becomes a source of advantage.

Second Base: Develop the Basic Skills!

Metal bats "feel" different, and carbon-graphite feels even more different from wood. That satisfying "crack" of the bat becomes a "ping" or a "clink." If you're used to wood, it takes some time to get comfortable. The same is true of the new oversized gloves. They feel fat and awkward at first. Sometimes competent players find they actually play worse (for a while) than they did with the old equipment, and some will even go back to the old equipment despite the potential of eventually playing better. The basic skills of baseball are still as fundamental as ever—throwing, hitting, and catching—but sometimes players need to relearn them in the context of the new equipment.

Joey almost quit the team because he couldn't use his dad's glove and bat. He was comfortable with them, and more important, he knew that he played fairly well with them. Using the new equipment, however, was awkward and meant playing worse for a while. Joey felt like he was starting over, learning how to catch and hit. No one wants to feel incompetent or to have to relearn the basic skills.

The *basic skills* of selling haven't changed—persuasive skills, prospecting, qualifying, presenting, closing, among others—but many of the tools have changed that we use to apply those skills more effectively. Remember "smokestacking"? Today, many salespeople are instead using computerized demographic data to target prospects or leads with the greatest potential for business. Sales presentations have changed from flip charts and black-and-white overheads to computer-generated color slide shows and multimedia presentations. Even the venerable paper planner and appointment calendar is falling to the notebook or handheld computer for better management of "To-Do's" and follow-ups.

The basic skills of selling haven't changed—and probably never really will—but the environment or context in which we're now applying them has changed. Salespeople, especially the most experienced and those with long records of success, will need to be retrained on how to meld their good selling skills with the new technologies of selling. An important distinction is that the task is *not* just one of teaching them how to *operate* computers, automation software, electronic mail networks, and the like. The real task will be educating them on how to use them as effective selling tools, tools that help salespeople develop better sales strategies and tactics and create competitive advantage.

This new way of selling will be awkward at first; for some people there may even be an initial drop in sales productivity as new ways of doing things are relearned. Like Joey, many will invariably "hit the wall"; that is, they'll reach a point at which they are ready to go back to the old tried and true methods. They still want to know, "Why can't we sell the same way we did five and ten years ago and get the same results?" The manager's task is going to be answering the question and helping manage that change through a new focus on sales strategies and tactics.

THIRD BASE: CREATE WINNING STRATEGIES AND TACTICS!

A definition of successful *strategies* is "the allocation and positioning of available resources in the optimum manner to produce the desired results most efficiently, that is, meet established goals."

> *Don't try to explain this to nine-year-olds. They aren't impressed. Their parents aren't either. Most of the strategy in Little League comes down to figuring out who plays where and arranging the batting order. Terry catches well but can't throw; he's definitely first-base potential. Mike catches well and throws straight; he's a shortstop. Billy catches well and throws well but has no idea what's going on. Put him in left or right field (whichever is closer to the dugout so I can yell to him to wake up before the ball hits him). Mark throws slow but straight; he's a starting pitcher. And so it goes.*
>
> *A game strategy is also based on some amount of baseball knowledge and experience—often painfully acquired. For example, kids more often hit balls to the infield between first and second. Fly balls usually go to center or right fields. Throwing to third more often scores a run for the other team (kids miss a lot!).*
>
> *I learned that, generally, if you can get the right players in the right positions that maximize their strengths and minimize their weaknesses, you start to win. Figuring that out before it's too late in the season is management strategy.*

To repeat, the definition of successful *strategies* is "the allocation and positioning of available resources in the optimum manner to produce the desired results most efficiently, that is meet established goals." In creating a successful sales organization, our salespeople are our strategy! In other words, *management strategy* is positioning and allocating our salespeople to take maximum advantage of their strengths and working with them to correct their weaknesses. As they develop, we need to be prepared to reposition them.

Developing the sales reps must be a key element of a management strategy. That means *knowing* what they're strong in and what they're not, and putting plans in place to address their abilities. "Trades" (firing low-performers and hiring what is hoped will be better replacements) should be a last-resort option because of the cost and time necessary to get a new rep up to speed.

> *In Little League, a lot of the tactics comes down to where to throw the ball when it's hit to you. Tactics are situational and they require precise execution. For example, if the ball is hit to you, and there are two outs, and a runner is on third, where do you throw the ball? (Hint: The answer is not "to the second baseman 'cause he's my brother.")*
>
> *The thing is, tactics can be dangerous when you don't have the basic skills or fundamentals of the game firmly in place. When Craig stepped up to bat and got his very first hit, he remembered his dad's words just before the game: "Make me proud, Craig. Go out there and hit a home run!" It wasn't that much of a hit, really, just a dribbler between first and second. Craig, remembering his mission, however, applied tactics as he rounded first, took a hard left turn, and headed for home — directly across the pitcher's mound. Generally speaking, Craig had the right idea; he just didn't see why second and third base were necessary steps.*

To look at it another way, salespeople have two — and only two — variables which they can control in selling, on which they can be coached by sales managers: *strategies* and *tactics* (quality and execution). Everything else is either fixed, such as products and territories, or under someone else's control, such as product specification and perhaps price.

> **Tactics are the way we use our sales "equipment" combined with our "basic skills" of selling to respond most effectively to each of the sales tasks and situations within a clearly defined sales process.**

In short, the tactical job of a sales manager is assuring that everyone understands and uses the sales process and knows "where to throw the ball" and the right "play" to make for any sales situation.

HOME PLATE: TEAMWORK

> *You would think that the importance of teamwork would be obvious in Little League. You would think. At the age of nine, unfortunately, three-quarters of your players firmly believe that they are destined for at least a college baseball scholarship if not a pro career by the time they're sixteen.*

Bart wasn't one of my players; he played for the White Sox. (Thank God for small favors!) He's destined for baseball stardom or federal prison, whichever comes first. Bart played for Bart — and he was a nine-year-old phenom. When Bart hit the ball, he always went for home, even when the base coach tried to hold him up at second or third. He usually made it, too. He scored a lot of runs, and his team won a lot of games because of him, for a while.

The other players soon resented that the "rules" didn't necessarily apply to Bart in the same way they did to them because Bart was a star. He didn't have to listen to the coaches. If Bart missed a practice, it wasn't a problem. Bart played any position he wanted. Bart was essential to winning, and they were not. After a while, the team began to lose despite its star.

It wasn't really Bart's fault. He was only doing what almost any nine-year-old would do in the same situation. The blame was with the coaches who let Bart stop being part of the team. Instead of creating a leader, they created two teams: "Bart" and "The Rest." The message is that you can win with just your stars for a while, but not forever.

As sales managers we like to focus on our stars. Not only are they bringing in revenue, which usually translates into cash in our pockets, but also they're more fun to be with. They're successful and enthusiastic; they don't have problems, except perhaps the good kind ("I could sell more if I had a bigger territory!"). More important, they're a lot like us. We identify with their success because we had it as well when we were out there selling.

Because of that tight psychological connection, we may identify so closely with them that we have a harder time requiring them to live by the same rules, policies, and procedures we've established for the other members of the sales team. Didn't we get special treatment in our days of selling stardom? Isn't that one of the rewards of being a star? And what if they became unhappy and quit; how would I make my numbers then?

Selling today is rapidly being redefined as a *team sport*. The teams are not just the sales unit but also account teams, regional teams, and even the field and the corporation as another team. The new *enabling technologies* of sales automation are electronically tying together sales and support teams—all sharing customer data, competitive information and strategies, marketing and leads data, product information, and so forth. *These teams and the technologies work, however, only when everyone shares the same rules, strategies, tactics, skills, and equipment.*

The point is that we, as managers, must create teams as the means to implement our strategies and tactics most effectively. We have to retain our faith and knowledge that in the long run a well-managed team with strong mutual synergy will produce greater results than any collection of individuals. But the season seems so short! We either resist the temptation of short-term, uncontrolled selling (letting the stars do their own thing), or we shall see the eventual disintegration of our team-building efforts.

**The day of the sales star is ending,
replaced by top performers who are leaders within their teams.**

SECOND INNING: YOU GOTTA HAVE A GAME PLAN

Buddy is a real baseball coach. He was once the coach of the junior varsity team at a high school, and he got paid for it. That makes him a professional, in a way. Buddy asked me to help him coach the Pirates, his Babe Ruth League team of thirteen- to fifteen-year-olds. I said yes. I'm an idiot.

We had a great year. The Pirates won the town championship, and Buddy and I were named coaches of the "All-Star" team. (My wife is still laughing about that one!)

Buddy taught me about coaching teenagers. Managing little kids was easy by comparison. You teach little kids how to hit and where to stand; you tell them when to run and where to throw the ball, and you encourage them a lot. That's about it.

Teenagers are different—really different! Young teenage males on any given day vary in age from two to thirty. Of the sixteen players on the Pirates' roster, I counted at least 256 different personalities during a single game. And the parents in the stands have been replaced by teenage girls. This is why the boys usually put winning the game as second priority to "looking good."

During one game, I personally took Tom (who used to be known as Tommy the previous year) to the hospital after he caught a line drive to an unfortunate and very painful part of his body. This incredibly unfortunate and painful event happened as Tom was occupied "posing" at first base for his girlfriend, the adoring Lisa. This was definitely not "looking good." Lisa shouldn't have laughed.

Buddy explained the difference to me between coaching young kids and coaching hormonally-influenced teenagers. Mothers and fathers of America, listen up! It's not pretty, but you need to hear it!

According to Buddy, Little Leaguers need to be told what to do—where to stand, how to hit, and all that. They even want and expect to be told what to do. Teenagers, however, unswervingly believe that they already know precisely what to do and when and how to do it. They know that they have progressed "beyond coaching." (This is especially amazing to see when they have never played the particular sport before, but it is still an absolute truism!) And of course, the teenage ego is a fragile and precious thing. In the words of Buddy, "You don't really lead these teenage boys. The best you can do is point them in the right direction and 'herd' them that way. They'll go that way if they think you know what you're talking about." Then he'd spit.

You can't lead older players with basic skills and tactics. You "herd" or motivate them in the right direction by having a *game plan*.

Vince Lombardi, the coach of the legendary Green Bay Packers in the 1960s, was so successful leading the Packers because he did two things so very, very well. First, he understood the importance of having a *game plan*; and second, he understood that the game was won *play by play*. Lombardi established leadership and "herded" his team in the direction he wanted them to go by having a solid game plan before each contest. Following hours of painstaking review of game films and scouting reports, he could accurately brief his players on the competition's strengths and weaknesses and its probable game plan; he could set and clearly communicate his strategy for success, namely, how he planned to deploy the Packers' skills and abilities in order to win and how the team needed to improve before the game. During the actual game, he sent in specific plays (*tactics*) as he watched the game progress. Vince Lombardi was a leader, and the Packers won because he did his job and he let the players do theirs. He coached and they executed, play by play.

It has often amazed me how much salespeople are like my baseball players. Sales trainees and relatively inexperienced sales reps really need and want coaching to develop solid skills and *tactics*. At that stage of their development, they need to be trained continuously and reminded of what we think of as "the basics."

Most sales managers are fairly comfortable with this kind of managing and coaching, if only because those skills are firmly established and come easily. But salespeople, like Little Leaguers, someday grow up to become "experienced sales professionals" with a whole different attitude and set of needs.

Experienced salespeople are looking for their managers to provide a *game plan* for success. "Give me the strategy, boss; call in a play when you see a way to do things better, and let me do the rest!" Like Lombardi's game plan, the sales game plan needs to be based on solid market knowledge and up-to-date competitive information distilled by a sales manager into a "playbook" of successful tactics.

Too many sales managers are excellent tactical or skill coaches, very effective with young salespeople but viewed by experienced reps as a bit of a nuisance. It's not surprising they see us this way because few if any of us managers were trained to be anything else.

For many of us, the coaching and managing skills with which we're the most familiar and know how to use the best don't really apply to the most important segment of our sales force. To find out where you stand, ask yourself this question:

> **"Do my most experienced people think that I have a real game plan for success? If so, could they tell me what it is?"**

An effective manager, then, needs to become a chameleon — leading inexperienced salespeople with solid tactical coaching and leading those with experience by providing a solid game plan, sending in play tactics as the sale progresses, and letting the sales reps execute. In short, "You gotta have a game plan!"

THIRD INNING: WHO WINS THE GAME, ANYWAY?

Chris is a nice guy. He's in his mid-thirties and holds a good job as an engineering manager. He's also a fanatical Little League coach. I think Chris missed some things when he signed up to be a coach, such as, this isn't professional baseball. When Chris looks out from the dugout, I firmly believe that he actually sees a stadium with 50,000 fans. It must be true because otherwise I can't understand why Chris gets so worked up over a kids' game and why he spends so much time yelling at and berating his young players when they lose. I think Chris is confused about who really wins the game.

Now I've been known to get worked up a time or two myself. I even got thrown out of a game once for arguing with an umpire and kicking dirt on his shoes. (I'm not very proud of it. The umpire was thirteen and had on brand-new Reeboks. Still, it seemed like the right thing to do at the time!)

My point isn't that Chris shouldn't be that upset over a kids' game. It's not even that Chris shouldn't be upset at all. It's just that Chris takes losing so personally—and takes it out on his players—because he feels that he lost!

> **A manager is not a player. A manager doesn't *directly* win or lose. Only players can win or lose. The manager's *only* job on the team is to help the players win! If the players win, the manager wins.**

Sometimes the hardest thing for a sales manager to accept is that he or she is no longer a player—in other words, a sales representative. We no longer have the ability to win or lose at selling. We become winners *only* when our salespeople win. In short, we're out of the game, kicked upstairs, and not allowed on the field of play, except occasionally to give some advice or encouragement. We get to pick the team, create the game plan, and send in plays. That's it.

When I was a young sales trainee, my first manager was Jeff. I spent hours in Jeff's office every time I made a mistake in a sales call or lost a deal. He kept the door shut to muffle the yelling. He often reminded me that he had real doubts if I was going to make it in sales, that I just didn't "get it," and that I was making him look bad. I went home at night, scared to tell my wife that I was probably going to be fired soon. Even so, I did make quota but mostly out of fear and desperation. Funny, I didn't feel like much of a "winner" despite my good performance, and I quit soon after. Jeff and I both lost.

There are sales managers who look "up" and sales managers who look "down." "Up" managers spend their lives looking *upward* in the organization chart toward their manager and their manager's managers. They worry about whether they're perceived as a "winner" — and suitable for promotion. Their salespeople had better perform, or *they're going to find others who will*!

"Down" managers focus *downward* in the organization chart toward their salespeople. They understand that their own success is solely a *reflection* of the success of their salespeople. Their task is to make them winners — winners who stay with the organization year after year and only get better. Promotions for the manager will take care of themselves. These managers perceive themselves as a resource, a mentor.

> Chris and his team won the town championship three years in a row with virtually unbeaten teams. He also had to draft an entire new team each year because so many of his players quit the sport after a year with him. Winning didn't make them "winners." It did stop them, however, from realizing their future potential in the game.

Whether management tends to look "upward" or "downward" also tells a lot about a company's overall sales success and the way the salespeople sell. Don't we hear a lot today about making salespeople "customer-focused"? Isn't the real measure of a sales rep's success the success of the customer? Isn't it *that success* that keeps the customer buying from us?

Salespeople also need to look "downward" toward their customers and prospects to achieve long-term success. Sales and corporate success needs to start at the bottom — at the customer — and flow upward to the salesperson, to the manager, and to all levels of the company.

Conclusions?

Only salespeople win or lose the game. Managers help make it happen! Customer-focused salespeople come from salesperson-focused sales managers.

FOURTH INNING: PLAY THE BENCH

Even in youth baseball, where everyone gets to play at least a minimum number of innings, there are "bench warmers." Managers want to win and thus want to play their "stars" as much as possible. It makes sense to me, or at least it did until my son, Tim, asked me how the bench warmers were ever going to get any better if they didn't get to play.

I told Tim that that was what practices were for. He didn't think it was the same. It made me think about how much attention we really pay to our "bench warmers" — even in practices.

Baseball managers and sales managers have something in common. Both spend most of their time and attention on their stars. The problem is that they're the ones who need us the least.

If we're not focusing on our sales stars, then we're focusing on "the hopeless" — the sales reps who just are not making the grade and who often have more of an *attitude* problem than a *skills* problem. The fact is that we can't really do much for them either.

The people who do need us and who can benefit from what we have to offer are "the bench."

Who's on the bench? The majority of the sales force! They're the *average* players or sales reps who are "good" players but rarely make either the big play or the big sale. Most, at least, do want to be better than they are. As managers, however, we find that they're not nearly as much fun to work with as top performers; in fact, we tend to criticize their performance more than develop it.

The bench needs to be — and can successfully be — developed into solid performers, the ultimate foundation of a sales team.

Consider the impact of ignoring "the bench" when we implement SFA or train our people in opportunity management. The focus always seem to be on the "stars." They are the ones always picked for focus groups and asked to evaluate new methodologies, hardware and software, and so on. The problem is, however, the new systems are really not for them. They are the ones who need them the least — and who least appreciate what the people on the bench really need!

Too many sales effectiveness programs and ideas fail because they are inadvertently focused on exactly the wrong people.

FIFTH INNING: LOVE THOSE PRACTICES

A baseball game isn't supposed to be a learning experience. It's the time when you execute what you've learned well. That's why even professional teams filled with true athletic stars practice every single day. Practice is the only way to develop and hone skills to produce competitive advantage, but even the pros hate to practice.

Salespeople *really* hate to practice—*especially* the sales "stars." They complain (and too many managers agree) that training takes valuable time away from selling. Many say that making sales calls is the best way to learn to sell. Losing sales because we're not as good as we ought to be seems counterproductive at best, and it leaves a trail of dissatisfied prospects. How much value is coaching after a bad sales call?

I watched a documentary about Walter Payton, the great running back of the Chicago Bears. In his career, Payton ran for almost 17,000 career yards. He was only 5'10" and weighed just 175 pounds, but he could bench press 400 pounds and leg press over 700! Payton's success came from his incredible level of preparation; he practiced and conditioned incessantly. It was his quest for perfect execution that leveraged his outstanding performance on game day. To gain those 17,000 yards, Walter Payton had probably less than twenty game "opportunities" each year of his career—and he practiced to make every one of them count. Amazing!

This morning a sales manager called to let me know he had decided to cancel the upcoming sales training because the salespeople protested they just couldn't afford the time out of the field. Amazing!

What do these two "amazing" things have in common? I hear again and again in sports that training and preparation are the keys for athletic success on game day. World-class athletes invest days, weeks, and even months of nonstop training and planning for *each competition!* In the business of selling, however, it's often just the opposite. Training and planning are a luxury, not a necessity. In short, for salespeople every day is apparently game day. But should it be that way?

Consider what the true purpose of sales training ought to be: (1) to make the sales cycle as short as possible by helping salespeople find the best business opportunities, and then (2) to *enable* them to better work and close each "deal" as quickly and efficiently as possible. Sounds like a good—and potentially very profitable—investment: sell more with the same or even less resources! *Constant practices are the key to achieving perfect execution.*

"But wait," you say, "selling isn't a physical sport! It's a nice analogy, but the two are not the same!" No, selling is as much a physical endeavor as any athletic event, but the *mind is the muscle of selling*. The mind's abilities, conditioning, and sharpness on each selling "game day" ultimately determine success or failure.

You might keep this in mind: salespeople most resist training, planning sessions, and coaching exactly when they need them the most, but ultimately these are the only tools we can really use to improve sales performance.

> **The best prepared and the best conditioned become the best motivated who will execute the most perfectly to win!**

SIXTH INNING: PLAY BY THE RULES

Rules are fine as long as they apply to everybody. It's OK as long as the umpire keeps the strike zone consistent, but not when it seems to change from batter to batter. Nobody really minds early morning baseball practices on a Sunday unless some people (especially the stars) don't show up, and the coach doesn't seem to care. It ruins team morale when, after everyone is taught to hit a certain way or play a position in a specific way, some players seem to get to do things any way they want to do them.

After a while, nobody is following the rules at all, the coach is yelling with frustration, and the team is losing.

In some sales organizations, the "rules" don't seem to apply to everyone in exactly the same way. Some basic examples are practices, sales reporting, coaching sessions, and adhering to new policies and procedures.

It becomes more critical when the top performers are exempt from team selling and planning or adopting new sales methods and technologies that have potential benefit for the entire team. What if the top performer doesn't want to use our sales process or complete the assessments and planning in STRATEGY MAPPING? What if this star salesperson refuses to use sales automation technology? The answer, of course, is that after a while no one uses them, and no one follows the rules at all.

> **When the rules aren't the same for everyone, a sales manager risks losing everything: respect, authority, and especially his or her potential to become a manager who creates a winning team.**

SEVENTH INNING: MOTIVATION— GET THROUGH TO THE PLAYERS

Coaching kids in youth baseball teaches you a lot about getting through to people. Take motivation. I learned that "negative motivation" (yelling) often gets compliance ("You were out of position! Next time do what I tell you or I'll ... !!!"), but it rarely brings about long-term behavioral changes—especially when the kids quit the team. Brilliant motivational speeches, while entertaining, rarely produce more than the most short-term results. ("Win one for the Gipper!") By the same token, the "Dr. Feel Good" approach ("Hey, that's OK. You'll hit one next time!") isn't always the best approach either.

I finally learned to quit focusing on my management style and start focusing on my players' learning styles. For example, to change behaviors, some kids respond best to a firm set of rules consistently applied; other kids really respond to a manager who has faith in them and supports them; still others respond more to team (peer) pressure than anything else.

Motivating the sales force is one of the most fundamental and difficult tasks of any sales manager, and there are as many techniques as there are managers. Most of us feel that our people are generally "created in our own likeness"; that is, what motivates us will motivate them. Sometimes it works and sometimes it doesn't. So trying to figure out the right combination to most effectively motivate a salesperson can be an exercise in real frustration.

A different way to look at motivation is to use the three **prime motivators**: *power, relationships*, and *security*. Understanding and identifying these prime motivators helps sales managers decide which motivational techniques will work with which salespeople. Remember, different motivators work for different sales reps.

1. POWER

Money is power; promotion is power; recognition is power. *Power players* are naturally attracted to sales because no other profession offers better opportunities to excel and reap these rewards.

Recognition.

Power players are those who visibly want and "appreciate the best things in life": fine cars, a big home, and other perks. Many share a drive to be "number one" or express a clear intention to achieve promotion as quickly as possible.

Motivational Technique.

Quid pro quo Management. In other words, "you do (or sell) this much for me, and I'll make this happen for you." Offer money, recognition, corporate visibility, or promotion potential.

"I want and expect you to be the leader." It's important to keep in mind, however, that not all successful salespeople are "power" motivated!

2. RELATIONSHIPS

Some salespeople are team players; that is, they're most energized and motivated by being *a part of successful teams* and by working *with others*, such as other salespeople and customers.

Recognition.

A salesperson driven by the relationship motivator clearly values *personal* customer and company relationships. He or she likes recognition for quality of work and for being a team player. This person wants to be appreciated and liked for his or her efforts.

Motivational Technique.

Appeal to the salesperson's need for belonging: "I need you on the team; I know I can count on you to come through; the team (sales team, company) really needs your contribution; together we can make this happen!"

3. SECURITY

It seems like a contradiction in terms. Why would anyone who values security become a sales rep? New reps, however, are often most worried about just making quota to prove they can do and keep their job. An experienced salesperson may be more concerned about maintaining past earning levels and lifestyle than about becoming "number one" or being seen as a team player. And sadly some people are satisfied just to be average and achieve the minimum required.

Recognition.

Security-driven salespeople sometimes show inconsistent activity and energy levels; they don't seem to respond to traditional "positive" motivators, such as recognition or promotion.

Motivational Technique.

Managing with fear may only make things worse ("If you don't make the numbers this month...."), except perhaps as a last resort. Still, motivating this salesperson requires a firmer management style with clearly set requirements for goals and the tasks necessary to achieve them. Management expectations, however, need to be combined with a clear willingness to provide a reasonable level of support. In short, "I'll do everything I can to help you if you're giving me 100%—but remember I'm not going to do it for you!"

EIGHTH INNING: PULLING THE PITCHER

It's always a hard call for a baseball coach. The pitcher isn't throwing strikes, the other team is hitting home runs, and the players and parents can't understand why you haven't pulled him out.

On the one hand, if you leave him in, he may become so discouraged that he'll never pitch again or even quit the team (besides losing you the game). On the other hand, he won't grow and improve if you pull him too soon. He just might develop into a great pitcher if you give him more of a chance. Maybe you should just go out to the mound and talk to him.

With salespeople (they're all pitchers, by the way), sales managers sometimes have to make the same kinds of decisions. When a salesperson is not getting the job done, how many trips to the mound do you make? How long do you leave him in the game before you pull the plug and let him go? What do you say to your own manager who wants to know when you're going to make a change?

Then there's the guilt factor. If you pull (read "fire") the rep, well, nobody wants to put somebody else out of work. And you wonder if you could have turned things around. Besides, breaking in a new rep is a pain with a learning period before you see much performance. And management still wants to know what you're going to do to correct the problem.

Volumes have been written on this most difficult and often painful topic. In Little League, the game isn't long enough for complicated "should I, shouldn't I" analyses; the same is true of selling. So let's cut to the chase.

Before you "pull the pitcher," ask two questions. Unless you can answer "yes" to both, then it's probably time to "pull the pitcher."

1. **Is the sales rep willing to change?** Is he or she open to coaching, to learning, to trying new ideas?

2. **Is the sales rep capable of change?** In other words, does the person possess the fundamental *ability* to do the job the way we want it done?

Todd really wanted to be a pitcher. He practiced day and night on his own and with his dad. He was the most "coachable" player I ever had—always willing to listen and try to do what he was taught. Todd deserved a chance to pitch for the team, and he got it. That's when we realized he had a problem: Todd couldn't reach the plate. At that point in his development, Todd's arm just wasn't strong enough to consistently pitch a ball that far. He had the willingness to learn but not the ability to deliver. It was time to pull the pitcher!

Andy did it his way. His dad taught him to pitch, and that was the way he was going to do it. Andy had an arm like a rocket, but he was wild. We could fix that, but he wouldn't listen. Andy's pitches went all over the place. He had real ability, but he wasn't willing to learn. It was time to pull the pitcher!

This approach works well for salespeople too.

NINTH INNING: DRAFTING — AND PICKING WINNERS

I've always thought that "drafting" players for youth baseball was a little silly. I can safely say that now because I'm retired from coaching. We ought to just divvy up the kids. You get who you get, and you do the best you can. Some years you win a lot, and some years you don't. But that's not how it works.

On a cold Saturday morning every March, all the coaches troop out to the ball-field behind the middle school to watch "tryouts." (And in New Hampshire, it's always a cold Saturday morning.) Once we're sufficiently frozen and we've watched some 400 kids hit, catch, and throw, we go down to the youth center for the "draft."

The first year, I didn't take it especially seriously. I drafted all of Casey's friends. I thought that would be fun. How did I know he didn't have any friends who could pitch? We lost a lot of games.

The second year, I paid more attention. I drafted kids who looked like "good ballplayers." I got fifteen good second basemen. No pitchers, no catchers. Another long season.

The third year, I drafted by position. I knew what I needed, and I drafted play-ers to fill those positions. Not perfect, but we had a very good season.

I realized that I hired salespeople in much the same way I drafted players, with almost identical results. As a new manager, I hired people I liked, people with whom I thought I would get along. I even hired a few friends. I paid for that.

When I got smarter, I hired "good salespeople." I looked for "solid" sales skills and con-sistent past success. I wanted some serious *sharks*. I got better results, but not great.

Finally, I took a lesson from baseball and started hiring by "position." Not unlike a ball team, I started to ask myself about the overall sales territories for which I was ultimately responsible. What was their makeup? Solid customer base or relatively unprospected? Large accounts or small? Industry types? Did I need "prospectors" or reps who knew how to develop existing large accounts?

I also took a look at my sales unit. Did I need an experienced leader or a less experienced but enthusiastic rep? What skills did I want to bring to my unit that could be cross-trained? What did I have to offer the person I hired?

The point here is that I learned that as a manager, I needed to do the same Market/Territory/Account Analysis I ask my salespeople to do, except that it is for my total assigned territory. As we've said over and over, "it's what you don't know that kills you!"

You can't hire the person you need if you don't know what you need!

There's also the issue of hiring "eagles" or "ducks." We all want to hire the high-flying, sharp-eyed, and top-performing "eagles"; and to avoid hiring the "ducks" who always seem to be "decoyed" away from the sale and get shot down a lot. Despite how good hiring a potential sales rep may look on paper — and even how well he or she interviews — how can you tell if he or she will perform up to expectations? The greatest responsibility of management has always been and always will be the selection and hiring of the best people. Ultimately, all business success comes down to how well we do it. And, as we all know, it's an incredibly difficult, sometimes frustrating job.

I've hired "eagles," and I've hired some "ducks." What surprised me was that some of the *sure-thing* hires turned out to be ducks, and some of the *risky hires* turned out to be eagles. It made me seriously wonder about my hiring skills until I realized that each one of my successful people had some things in common that I'd never directly looked for.

All of my "winners" proved to be *emotionally stable*; they were actually energized by the ups and downs of the sales roller coaster. They were all *idea people* with active minds and raging creativity, the kind of people you had to hold back, not push out the door. Finally, all of them *lived to play the selling game*. They saw sales, *more than making money*, as the greatest game of all. Every day was a new chance to play, to win or lose.

We don't develop these attitudes in our people; they're innate characteristics. They're either there or they're not. I can teach my people to sell effectively, but I can't make an eagle out of a duck.

POST-GAME WRAP-UP

So that's what I learned coaching Little League, and that's what Little League taught me about coaching sales reps. I'm finally retired from baseball, though. My sons, Casey and Tim, have finally reached the point where even they don't want Dad as a coach. Ah well! The good news is that managing goes on forever.

SALES MANAGERS' PERSPECTIVES

FEAR OF THE FUTURE

A few weeks ago I overheard a conversation between two sales executives during a break at their annual sales conference. One commented that the salespeople just didn't seem to be responding to his attempts to motivate them and create enthusiasm for the upcoming year. "What's wrong with them?" he asked.

The other executive thought for a moment and responded, "The problem is fear! They can't get motivated because they're uncertain about the future. They're not sure where we're going and what will happen to them." It turned out that the company was considering a merger, and although the negotiations were in an early stage, the rumors of acquisition and impending layoffs were already rife throughout the organization.

"Well, we don't dare tell them about the merger," said the first executive. "That would really get them unmotivated!"

"I think you're underestimating them," replied the second. "Let's be up-front with them and see what happens."

I never found out what finally happened, but I generally agreed with the second executive who wanted to lay the cards on the table — at least as much as possible. In today's environment of acquisitions, downsizing, and layoffs, our people have lost the security that "doing a good job" brought in the past. Fear of the future is the greatest de-motivator, especially when it is based on conjecture and rumor that are often worse than reality. People see themselves as "victims" of the company rather than team members, and their fears create the self-fulfilling prophecy of failure.

CHAPTER 8

THE SALES MANAGER'S SURVIVAL KIT

"The Sales Manager's Survival Kit" is a compendium of tools for sales managers and project team members. It includes tools for project planning and evaluation, a financial justification model, and copies of the STRATEGY MAPPING and other forms used throughout the book.

To enhance their usability, each of these forms and documents may also be found on the enclosed computer disk. All were created in Microsoft Word 2.0 on an IBM PC.

Toolkit Topics

1. Financial Justification
2. Field and Sales Effectiveness Survey
3. SFA Strategic Plan
4. Sales Needs Questionnaire
5. STRATEGY MAPPING Forms

1. FINANCIAL JUSTIFICATION

Probably the most frequently asked questions about sales automation are "How do we justify it?" and "Where do we look for a tangible return on the investment?"

The problem is that so many measures are *subjective*: better prioritizing of leads, providing greater value to customers, more effective sales reps, and so forth. Even the measure of an increase in sales is unreliable because there are so many other market factors involved.

Despite these inherent difficulties, it is at least possible to identify areas within the company that can be potentially affected and to calculate a *relative measure of the potential*. The following questionnaire and justification analysis are designed to view the *maximum potential benefit amount* which, in an ideal situation, might be attained. It is for the evaluator to apply a *level of confidence* percentage to each of the boldface result calculations in order to create a realistic assessment of the potential.

Obviously not all questions or calculations will apply to all companies or sales organizations. Also, the results of the calculations are really not meant to be totaled. Each potential dollar benefit should be allowed to stand on its own as a single area of potential.

(Note: Questions in this section are not necessarily numbered sequentially. Some have been grouped differently to be used more easily in the calculation section.)

Finally, remember that success is still found through better process and information enabled by technology. Results will come from better sales decisions made by smart people with the right information at hand. For all these reasons, there are no guarantees, but there is unlimited potential!

SALES AUTOMATION JUSTIFICATION ANALYSIS QUESTIONNAIRE

GENERAL INFORMATION:

Company: _____

Division: _____

ORGANIZATION:

Number of Regional/Area Sales Managers (2nd and 3rd line): _____

Number of Sales Managers (1st line): _____

Number of Sales Representatives: _____

Number of Regional Offices: _____

District/Branch Offices: _____

Sales representatives primarily work from:

_____ a company office

_____ home

FIELD AUTOMATION PROFILE:

Marketing

Q1: What percentage of sales comes from the following sources?

A. _____ % direct-marketing programs/trade shows

B. _____ % advertising/call-ins

C. _____ % referrals

D. _____ % existing customers

E. _____ % other (service, support, etc.)

100% total

Please estimate the sources of business by percentage. This information will be used in assessing the effectiveness and costs of lead development programs.

Q2: Company's total marketing programs budget for the last full year: $ _____

Please enter the overall budget amount allocated for all marketing programs, such as direct mail, telesales, advertising, and trade shows. This would not include the departmental budget, overhead expenses, or employee salaries.

Q4: Total number of sales leads for the last full year: _____

Referring to Q1, what was the total number of new leads or new opportunities from direct marketing?

Q7: Percentage of leads that reach the salesperson's desk and are followed up within 30 days:_____%

This question refers to leads that have been received, processed through fulfillment and/or prequalifying, and distributed to and received by field sales representatives. An important note: estimates given at the 1994 "Direct Marketing to Business" conference place this number between 8% and 11% across all industries.

Q8: Company's lead follow-up target goal: _____%

Referring to Q7, what is a *realistic* percentage of leads received by salespeople that *can* and *should* be directly followed up within 30 days?

Q9: Percentage of qualified sales leads that close:_____%

What is the approximate percentage of all leads received from all sources that have been qualified as *viable potential opportunities* and that do close within 12 months?

Q10: Average direct marketing program lead-response percentage:_____%

This question refers specifically to direct marketing programs. A typical response rate is generally 3% to 5% for this kind of marketing through return mail or call-in.

Q11: Percentage of leads that are qualified prospects: _____%

Of new sales leads received *from all sources*, what percent are qualified opportunities for new business within a 12-month time frame?

Q12: Marketing's target percentage for qualified leads: _____%

An increase of _____%

Sales

Q6: Annual company sales revenue for the last fiscal year: $ _____

Please use the sales revenue figure from the last completed fiscal year rather than estimates of current year attainment, unless a dramatic difference is anticipated. This is an important number for further analysis and is best based on conservative and accurate data.

Q5: Average dollar revenue per sale: $_____

Q13: Average quota revenue dollars objective per salesperson: $_____

What is the average annual quota assignment for a typical sales representative, not including the sales trainees?

Q26: Total number of sales representatives in this company/division: _____

Q14: Average length of sales cycle in months: _____

Sales cycle length is defined as the time from the *qualification* of a viable sales opportunity to the formal customer *commitment*.

Q15: Average number of sales calls made daily per salesperson: _____

Q16: Salesperson Time Analysis: What percentage of a salesperson's day is spent in the following activities?:

A. _____ % face-to-face with customers/prospects

B. _____ % other sales-generating activities

C. _____ % administrative/internal meetings

D. _____ % travel

E. _____ % other: _____

   100% total

The *Harvard Business Review* estimates that categories A and B (which reflect actual sales-generating activity) are a *maximum* of 60% for even the most efficient salesperson.

Q17: What is your target mix percentage for daily direct sales-generating activities by sales? _____ %

Referring to the previous question, what is a realistic goal for A and B activities?

Q19: Number of sales opportunities lost to competition during the last fiscal year: _____

Q20: Competitive Loss Analysis: The primary reasons for competitive losses were:

A. _____ % product or feature issues and/or pricing

B. _____ % not aware of opportunity or not until competition firmly entrenched

C. _____ % unaware of competitive activity or presence

D. _____ % lack of competitive knowledge or information

E. _____ % competitor more knowledgeable, better informed

Q21: What percentage of these losses could have become wins if the sales force had more up-to-date competitive data, strategies, and tactics for specific competitors and broader territory activity information: _____ %

Although this question calls for a subjective estimate, please respond with your highest confidence level for any previous year's deals that might not have been lost with better competitive intelligence.

Q22: What is the average annual dollar revenue value of a typical "Active Account"? $ _____

An "Active Account" is defined as one that has a recurring revenue stream. This may be through regular purchase of products, support services, etc., or long-term contracts. Typically, an Active Account's sales revenue is forecasted in total at the beginning of the year.

Q23: Sales representative annual "turnover" due to:

      A. _____ resignation/termination

      B. _____ territory realignment/account reassignment

      C. _____ employee transfer

      D. _____ promotion

      E. _____ other:_____

         _____ total:

As this question indicates, sales representative turnover results from more than resignations. *Turnover* is defined as any sales organizational changes that alter or modify account relationships. This information is important in determining how many accounts (and their potential revenue) may be placed at risk for competitive intrusion due to a lost personal relationship and loss or inaccessibility of account information.

Q24: Average number of active customers managed per salesperson: _____

Q25: Number of new sales representatives hired annually: _____

Q27: Number of current existing accounts lost to competition in last fiscal year:_____

Management

Q28: Average time to develop a sales trainee to full quota production: _____ months

Most companies average a 12- to 18-month training period for new sales hires.

Q29: Average percentage of quota attained by sales trainee during this period: _____%

Most industry figures estimate that during the training period, typically 12–18 months, a sales trainee will sell approximately 50% of that expected of an on-quota sales rep.

Q31: Sales Manager Time Analysis: In what percentages do sales managers generally spend their time?

   A. _____% coaching sales reps/reviewing accounts/developing strategies and tactics

   B. _____% direct customer contact

   C. _____% administrative tasks

   D. _____% internal meetings (other than with sales reps)

   E. _____% other activities

      100% total

Q30: How much could trainee quota attainment be improved over this percentage with increased management attention (if time were available)?_____% increase

Q32: Average sales manager's annual income: $_____

Sales managers' earnings will be used to calculate the cost of sales management time.

Q33: Average number of sales reps managed by a sales manager: _____

Q34: Estimate the potential percentage impact on sales revenues of a sales manager enabled with better information (competitive data, comprehensive account profile, sales progress, and forecast information) to improve the following, given enough additional time to do so:

   A. _____% advancing or helping close the sale

   B. _____% developing territory or unit strategies

   C. _____% improve sales rep prioritization and business focus

   D. _____% directing reps away from "no-win" opportunities, moving "stalled" deals

   E. _____% increased direct customer contact

Q35: Overall, how much could sales revenues potentially increase (as a percentage) due to this increase in managerial focus and effectiveness? _____%

The average percentage estimates from Q34 may be used to provide this estimate.

Q36: Have sales been lost in the past year due to a lack of internal communication, for example, between salespeople selling to different divisions of large accounts, between sales and support personnel, etc.? If yes, how much revenue might have been generated by these opportunities? $ _____

Q37: What is the estimated or assumed accuracy of forecast data as received by first-line managers directly from the sales representatives?_____%

What would the impact be of increasing accuracy by 20%? By 50%?

The second question ("impact") does not require a numeric answer. Please attempt to identify areas within the organization that would be positively affected by an improvement in overall forecast accuracy. These may include:

- **manufacturing/distribution**
- **support staffing**
- **financial market credibility**
- **corporate expansion/contraction**
- **new product development and marketing**

JUSTIFICATION CALCULATION

Based upon the answers provided in the questionnaire, estimates of the optimal potential of sales automation to improve overall sales performance can be provided, keeping in mind that many additional internal and market factors will influence actual results achieved.

This analysis is meant to suggest areas within sales and marketing where the most significant financial benefits of sales automation can be found.

C1: Total percent of sales revenue generated from lead marketing: _____ %

    Calculation: **Q1 A + B + C**

This calculation indicates the percentage of total new business that is generated annually from direct marketing programs, trade shows, and advertising, that is, as a result of corporate marketing programs.

C2: Total revenue generated by lead marketing: $_____

    Calculation: **C1 x Q6**

Annual corporate revenues are multiplied times the percent of sales generated by direct marketing programs to indicate the dollar revenue produced by these programs.

C3: Actual number of sales leads actively followed up by the direct sales force: _____

    Calculation: **Q4 x Q7**

Total number of direct marketing sales leads received is multiplied by the percentage of leads estimated that are actively followed up by salespeople within 30 days of receipt.

C4: Cost/Lead Generated: $_____

    Calculation: **Q2 ÷ Q4**

The cost per lead generated by direct marketing is calculated by dividing the total annual marketing programs expenditure or budget by the total number of sales leads received.

C5: Cost/Lead Followed-up: $_____

    Calculation: **Q2 ÷ C3**

The cost per lead actively followed up by sales within 30 days is calculated by dividing the cost of the total annual marketing programs by the previously computed number of leads followed up. This number may be contrasted with the cost per lead generated and produces a more realistic look at the actual marketing cost of generating a sales lead, not including the costs of sales time or expense.

C6: Potential value of improving sales lead follow-up: $ _____

    Calculation: **(Q4 x Q7 x Q5) x Q9 = N (current revenue production from leads)**

    Calculation: **(Q4 x Q8 x Q5) x Q9 = P (potential revenue production from leads)**

    Calculation: P – N = Potential revenue growth from better lead follow-up

What is the potential added revenue value of increasing the percentage of total leads that are actively followed up by salespeople within 30 days of receipt? One way of viewing this is by first calculating current revenue production from leads: *leads received* times *current percentage of follow-up* times *average revenue per sale* then multiplied by the *percentage of qualified leads estimated closed*. The calculation is repeated substituting the *lead follow-up target goal* for the current follow-up percentage. The net difference between the two results in potential of revenue growth through increasing lead follow-up.

This calculation does *not* address the potentially far greater benefits of not only following up a greater percentage of leads received but using SFA to prioritize and select leads with greater probability of closing business.

C7: Potential marketing budget savings by improved target marketing: $ _____

    Calculation: **Q2 x (Q11 x Q10) = B ($ budget currently on target)**

    Calculation: **Q2 x (Q12 x Q10) = P (potential $ budget on target)**

    P – B = Savings or funds

    Calculation: Result is savings or funds available for additional programs

Marketing budget savings is defined as current money spent on nonproductive marketing efforts that might be redirected to programs with increased potential for generating qualified leads. The percent of the current marketing budget that is "on target" (generating qualified leads) is calculated by taking the *annual direct marketing budget* multiplied by the *average direct marketing lead response percentage* times the *percentage of qualified leads received*. Substituting marketing's goal or *target percentage for qualified leads received* and subtracting these two results indicates marketing dollars "saved" (not wasted).

C8: Sales represenative time spent in direct selling activities:

a:_____%, b: _____ hrs./wk.

Calculation: **Q16: A + B = T (% time)**

Calculation: **(2000 hours x T) ÷ 48 weeks = (hours/week)**

The percentage of a salesperson's time spent on direct revenue-generating activities is calculated by adding the *face-to-face time* estimated to the estimate of *other sales-generating activities*.

The actual hours per week of direct selling activity is determined by multiplying this percentage by *2000 hours*, the approximate number of work hours annually available to a rep for selling activity and divided by *48 weeks* (the number of weeks available annually for selling after vacations, holidays, company meetings, etc.).

C9: Value of each hour of selling time toward revenue quota production: $ _____

Calculation: **(Q13 ÷ 48) ÷ C8(b) = H**

Taking a salesperson's average *annual sales quota or revenue goal* and dividing it by the *average annual hours spent by a sales rep in direct selling* produces the relative dollar value of each hour of sales time toward meeting annual goals and indicates the potential value of increasing available selling time by reducing time spent on nonproductive activities.

C10: Potential value of increasing sales direct selling time: $_____

Calculation: **T x 2000 hrs. = V (current time spent in direct selling activities)**

Calculation: **Q17 x 2000 hrs. = W (target for time spent in direct selling)**

Calculation: **W – V = Y**

(Y x C9) = R

R x Q26 x Q9 = Potential revenue

The potential impact of meeting the company's *target percentage mix for direct/indirect time* is illustrated by calculating the increased selling hours between *current* and *target* and multiplying the added hours times the hourly value of selling time. Multiplying this number times the total number of company salespeople times an overall sales effectiveness percentage (*closing percentage*) returns a valuable indicator of potential revenues through better sales time allocation.

This number is only meant to show the sales dollar value of time. Added sales are the result of how well sales and management utilize it.

Another way of viewing this result is as *adding additional salespeople to the organization without additional cost*. Take a typical salesperson's *average weekly direct sales hours* times *48 weeks* for an annual number. Divide this into the total number of *hours saved;* the result indicates the effective number of additional salespeople added to the sales force without cost or head-count increase.

C11: Potential increase in pipeline value: $_____

    Calculation: **Q4 x Q11 x Q9 x Q5 = D (current revenue value of qualified leads)**

    Calculation: **Q4 x Q12 x Q9 x Q5 = E (projected revenues with higher qualification)**

    Calculation: **E – D = Net sales revenue increase possible**

A viable approach to increasing sales revenues is through changing the composition of the sales pipeline or funnel. The objective is to increase the number of *qualified leads* within the pipeline rather than just the total number of leads available.

First compute the current revenue value of qualified leads in the existing pipeline by taking the *total leads received* times the *percentage of qualified leads* times the *qualified lead closing percentage* and then multiplying by the *average revenue per sale*. Repeat the calculation using marketing's *target percentage for qualified leads received*. The net difference between these two results illustrates the added revenue value of placing more qualified leads in the sales pipeline.

Although no specific value is calculated, there may be additional benefits to *replacing* poor quality leads with more qualified ones. A high percentage of poor quality leads *clogs the pipeline*, using up valuable sales time and expense.

C12: Potential sales dollar value of competitive intelligence: $ _____

    Calculation: **Q19 x Q5 = C (potential new revenue lost to competition)**

    Calculation: **C x Q21 (lost revenues that might have been avoided)**

In the justification questionnaire, managers are asked last year's number of competitive sales losses and the percentage of these which realistically might have been turned in to successful sales with better competitive intelligence. This calculation converts those answers into the additional revenues that might have been attained had such information been available.

C13: Active Accounts: Revenue at risk due to account transitions: $_____

Calculation: **Q22 x Q23 x Q24 = (Value of all accounts placed at risk through turnover last year)**

Existing accounts and current new sales opportunities become "at risk" to competitive intrusion whenever there is transition of field personnel through reassignment, territory realignment, or resignation. Personal customer relationships are jeopardized and valuable customer information, often critical to the sale or a continuing relationship, is lost. Given the number of actual *account turnovers* indicated, the *average annual revenue produced by an existing account* and the *average number of accounts managed per salesperson*, we can calculate the dollar amount of sales revenue placed "at risk" last year through account transition.

C13.1: Sales revenues lost to competition that had to be "recaptured" to net zero: $_____

Calculation: **Q27 x Q22**

When an existing account — one that produces a continuing revenue stream and has been forecasted as a high-probability element of current quota attainment — is lost to competition (through the lack of competitive intelligence, account transition, or other reasons), that revenue must be "recaptured" by finding additional or offsetting sales. In effect, the loss of such an account may be considered a sales quota increase.

This calculation presents the effective *sales quota increase* added last year to the sales organization's goals. The number of *competitive losses of existing accounts* is multiplied by the *average dollar revenue value of an existing account*.

C14: Potential revenue increases by sales trainees through increased

management attention and coaching: $_____

Calculation: **Q25 x Q13 x (Q29 + Q30) = K (total potential revenue attainment)**

Calculation: **K – (Q25 x Q13 x Q29) = Net potential sales increase**

Sales trainees represent a significant drain on the sales managers' time and resources. Trainee development is a critical long-term objective, but it takes time away from a manager's ability to focus on necessary short-term business. The only viable solution to this problem is to accelerate the return on investment through increasing overall revenue production by new salespeople. During the training period, SFA allows managers to provide greater focus and guidance with a reduced expenditure of time and resources.

To illustrate the potential value of trainee productivity to annual goals, we have taken the number of *new salespeople hired* last year, the *average quota attainment percentage*, and the *estimate of quota improvement* given to calculate the net potential trainee revenue that could be realized with increased management attention.

C15: Management time spent in direct selling activities: _____ hrs./wk.

    Calculation: **(Q31 (A + B)) x 40 hrs.**

Most sales managers agree that the best possible use of their time is in activities that have a direct impact on sales — specifically either face-to-face time with customers or in coaching the sales representatives. This calculation indicates the average number of hours per week that sales managers spend in these activities from the information provided.

C16: Cost value of management selling time: _____ /wk.

    Calculation: **(Q32 ÷ 50) x (Q31 A + B)**

C17: Cost value of management nonselling time: $ _____ /wk.

    Calculation: **(Q32 ÷ 50 ÷ 40) x (40 – C15)**

These two calculations — the cost values of management's selling and nonselling time — indicate how a company's investment in sales managers is being spent. The average income of a sales manager is divided by the percentages of time spent in both types of activities and a resultant dollar cost is calculated weekly.

C18: Potential overall increase in sales manager effectiveness: _____ %

    Calculation: **[Average of Q34] (A + B + C + D + E) ÷ 5**

The questionnaire asked for estimates of the impact of increased managerial effectiveness on sales revenues based on five criteria: (1) advancing stalled sales or closing assistance, (2) strategy development, (3) improving sales rep focus and priorities, (4) coaching, and (5) increased direct contact with customers. The *potential increase in sales manager effectiveness* is the average of the improvement percentages in these five areas.

C19: Potential revenue increase due to improved managerial effectiveness: $ _____

   Calculation: **Q35 x Q6**

Potential increases in managerial effectiveness are converted into a dollar revenue figure by taking the *effectiveness estimate* multiplied by last year's *annual revenue*. This indicates the amount that last year's sales might have been increased by managers' activities.

C20: Lost revenues due to poor internal communication and team selling: $ _____

   Calculation: **Q36**

On the questionnaire is the estimate of added revenues that might have been generated through improved team communications and selling efforts.

C21: Potential impact of improvements in forecast accuracy:

Areas of corporate-wide improvement potential from attaining greater accuracy in sales forecasts: (from questionnaire)

ALTERNATIVE MODELS

SALES GROWTH MODEL

There are simpler, less complex ways to look at justification for sales automation. The simplest is the "Sales Growth Model" that poses the question, "What increase in sales do we need to cover SFA costs and show a positive ROI?" This is also known as the *Sales Automation Confidence Question*. In other words, if it would take a 5% sales increase next year to achieve a one-year payback, do we feel confident that SFA could help the sales reps sell 5% more next year if we raised quotas by that amount? My advice is that if you can't answer "yes," don't automate.

Here's an example using a gross sales and net profit margin increase models:

FIGURE 8.1. GROSS SALES INCREASE

COST OFFSET

"What sales increase do we need to see to offset the costs of SFA and show positive ROI?"

 ## GROSS SALES INCREASE

EXAMPLE: 1 year full payback

1. SALESPERSON AVG. ANNUAL SALES	$1,000,000
2. ALLOCATED SFA COST	8,000
% GROSS INCREASE TO OFFSET	**.08%**

FIGURE 8.2. NET PROFIT INCREASE

COST OFFSET

"What sales increase do we need to see to offset the costs of SFA and show positive ROI?"

 ## NET PROFIT INCREASE

EXAMPLE: 1 year full payback

1. SALESPERSON AVG. ANNUAL SALES	$1,000,000
2. ALLOCATED SFA COST	8,000
3. PROFIT MARGIN	10%
% GROSS INCREASE TO OFFSET	**8%**

TRADITIONAL JUSTIFICATION METHOD

In the computer industry, as well as in many others, the "Traditional Justification Method" looks at two potential justification areas: *cost displacement* and *cost avoidance*. Surprisingly these have rarely been applied to sales automation justification, but they are as valid for SFA as they have been proven for the traditional business applications.

FIGURE 8.3. TRADITIONAL JUSTIFICATION METHOD

"Traditional" Justification Techniques

1. COST DISPLACEMENT

2. COST ALTERNATIVE WEIGHTING

To envision this model, consider a mythical company with two regional offices and ten branch offices staffed by managers, secretaries, administrators, and salespeople. As part of their automation strategy, the company adopts the *Virtual Office*. The company moves sales reps to home offices, closing all branch offices and leaving only the regional offices in place. Interestingly enough, companies that have actually done this have reported an 18 to 20% *bottom-line profit increase*, or more than enough to justify SFA.

Cost Displacement

FIGURE 8.4. COST DISPLACEMENT

COST DISPLACEMENT

⇒ **Virtual Office Model**

* **SUPPORT/ADMINISTRATIVE STAFF**
* **REAL ESTATE**
* **GENERAL OVERHEAD**

IMPACT: Up to 20% BOTTOM LINE

Cost displacement looks at the overhead resources in place today that may be unnecessary and potentially eliminated with sales automation technology. Typical displacements include the following:

Personnel: Can we eliminate or reduce:

1. Secretarial Staff _____ (branch office, support)

   Average annual salary + 25% benefits: $ _____

2. Administrative Staff _____ (order processing, lead fulfillment, etc.)

   Average annual salary + 25% benefits: $ _____

3. Other _____

   Average annual salary + 25% benefits: $ _____

Overhead: Can we eliminate or reduce:

1. Office rent: $ _____

2. Equipment costs or rentals: $ _____

3. Parking, utilities, insurance, etc.: $ _____

4. Other _____ : $ _____

5. Maintenance: $ _____

Cost Avoidance

COST AVOIDANCE

"AS-IS" Scenario

To achieve defined Strategic Goals utilizing <u>current methods</u>, identify additional (avoidable) costs in ...

   * **manpower**   *overhead

   * **systems**   *support

If cost displacement looked at the past (getting rid of what we already have), then cost avoidance looks at the future with this question: "If we do *not* automate, what additional costs will we incur?"

In other words, assume that we attempt to achieve our increasing sales goals with business as usual. For example, if we intend to add salespeople, there will likely be attendant administrative and overhead costs. If we increase business by 10% next year, what will be the additional personnel and overhead expenses that might be *avoided* if we automated?

Personnel: Will we add:

1. Secretarial Staff _____ (branch office, support)

  Average annual salary + 25% benefits: $ _____

2. Administrative Staff _____ (order processing, lead fulfillment, etc.)

  Average annual salary + 25% benefits: $ _____

3. Other _____

  Average annual salary + 25% benefits: $ _____

Overhead: Will we add:

1. Office rent: $ _____

2. Equipment costs or rentals: $ _____

3. Parking, utilities, insurance, etc.: $ _____

4. Other _____: $ _____

5. Maintenance: $ _____

2. FIELD AND SALES EFFECTIVENESS SURVEY

This is a simple, easy-to-use format for conducting regular general audits to assess usage levels and gain feedback data for system tuning and/or to identify personnel training issues. It is not meant to represent a full system audit but to be a quick management assessment tool.

FIELD EFFECTIVENESS SURVEY

Date: _____

User Name: _____

Location: _____

PROFILE

Level: _____ Executive _____ Field Manager _____ Sales _____ Other: _____

Type: _____ Corporate Office _____ Remote Company Office _____ Home/Virtual Office

Technical: _____ Desktop PC/LAN _____ Notebook PC/LAN _____ Notebook PC/Remote

PC Skills: _____ High _____ Intermediate _____ Novice

PRODUCTIVITY TOOLS

Sales Tool	Length of Use	Proficiency 10 high, 1 low	Rank 10=greatest value 1=least value	Freq. of Use M/D/W/O
1. Sales Automation				
2. E-Mail				
3.				
4.				
5.				
6.				
7.				
8.				
9.				

Notes:
Rank: Rank sales tool in order of greatest value to user's efficiency and productivity.
Frequency of Use: Multiple Daily, Daily, Weekly, Occasional

SALES AUTOMATION ASSESSMENT

Part I. General

1. What do you see as the greatest potential value of this productivity tool? Specificallly, what are the three most important ways it can help improve your productivity and effectiveness?

   A: _____

   B: _____

   C: _____

2. Describe how you utilize this tool on a daily basis:

3. What changes/improvements would you recommend to make this tool more valuable and useful?

Part II. Sales Automation Assessment

Since you first began using SFA, how has its use affected the following?

1. Responsiveness to customers' calls/requests:

   (a) improved greatly   (b) somewhat improved   (c) no change

   (d) decreased   (e) don't know   (f) not applicable

2. More effective time management and better territory organization:

   (a) improved greatly   (b) somewhat improved   (c) no change

   (d) decreased   (e) don't know   (f) not applicable

3. Quicker/easier access to customer information:

  (a) improved greatly   (b) somewhat improved   (c) no change

  (d) decreased   (e) don't know   (f) not applicable

4. Increased usable customer information available:

  (a) improved greatly   (b) somewhat improved   (c) no change

  (d) decreased   (e) don't know   (f) not applicable

5. Improved forecasting accuracy:

  (a) improved greatly   (b) somewhat improved   (c) no change

  (d) decreased   (e) don't know   (f) not applicable

6. Ability to identify high-potential opportunities and disconnect from low-potential:

  (a) improved greatly   (b) somewhat improved   (c) no change

  (d) decreased   (e) don't know   (f) not applicable

7. Easier/faster access to new leads:

  (a) improved greatly   (b) somewhat improved   (c) no change

  (d) decreased   (e) don't know   (f) not applicable

8. Increased leads handled or better focus on high-potential leads:

  (a) improved greatly   (b) somewhat improved   (c) no change

  (d) decreased   (e) don't know   (f) not applicable

9. What impact has this system had on your sales calls?

  _____ more calls   _____ fewer calls   _____ more effective

  _____ less effective   _____ increased face-to-face time   _____ not applicable

10. What is the overall impact of using this system on your time spent each day (for example, an increase or decrease in time spent reporting or logging information, etc.)?

  (a) improved greatly   (b) somewhat improved   (c) no change

  (d) decreased   (e) don't know   (f) not applicable

11. What are the specific features of SFA that you find the most useful?

   1.

   2.

   3.

   4.

   5.

12. What features/capabilities of the system do you find difficult or in which you need additional training or assistance?

Part III. Productivity Tool Assessment

Productivity Tool: _____

1. What do you see as the greatest potential value of this productivity tool? Specificallly, what are the three most important ways it can help improve your productivity and effectiveness?

   A: _____

   B: _____

   C: _____

2. Describe how you utilize this tool on a daily basis:

3. What changes or improvements would you recommend to make this tool more valuable and useful?

3. SFA STRATEGIC PLAN

There are many reasons why a company might report lack of satisfaction with the results of their SFA system. The most common reason, however, particularly in the first year, are goals and expectations that are either poorly defined or simply unachievable.

To be honest, misaligned expectations are rarely the fault of the project team, especially since many are venturing into new and somewhat uncharted waters. Still, when top management begins to ask for significant and measurable results shortly after sales automation implementation, they rarely find them. For this reason alone, many projects never get beyond the pilot phase.

The key is to create a strategic plan based on business solutions and not on technology with input and representation from all cross-functional groups interested in the project. The "Strategic Planning Model" is a basic framework for conducting this session.

AUTOMATION PROJECT STRATEGIC PLANNING MODEL: METHODOLOGY DESCRIPTION

The project assessment is a methodology to create and evaluate measurable and realistic short- and long-term goals that are attainable through the application of existing or identified resources. Goal-setting is done within the framework of attaining primary increases in sales enterprise effectiveness and secondary improvements in overall productivity. The primary working piece of the assessment is the establishing of short-term objectives, tracking, and subsequent evaluation of results on a regular timetable (ninety days to six months).

Rules:

Any element is limited to an absolute maximum of five subelements, for example, five long-term goals with no more than five subgoals for each.

Mission Statement and Long-Term Goals:

These are general statements of overall effectiveness/productivity goals within a rolling one- to five-year time frame. Long-term goals and target dates will change as short-term goals are met, exceeded, or delayed, as available resources increase or decrease, or as new and unanticipated obstacles surface.

Short-Term Objectives:

The short-term objectives and expectations comprise the basic working element of the automation assessment. Typically, short-term objectives will be evaluated, revised, and reissued on a ninety-day or six-month basis. Resources, obstacles, and requirements will be evaluated on the basis of each short-term plan and the creation of a tactical strategy. Short-term strategies dictate modifications to long-term goals. Short-term objectives consist of a maximum of five key effectiveness and productivity objectives with a maximum of five specific criteria for each.

Resources Available:

This section describes the "current" operational, technical, advisory (consulting, managerial, etc.), and financial resources available to the project *at the time of creation of the short-term objectives*, and includes the customer as well as the SFA vendor.

Obstacles:

The purpose of this section is to define forseeable obstacles to the project's success *at the time of creation of the short-term objectives*. Generally these will address technical, logistics, personnel, and financial obstacles. Resolution is addressed by the "Tactical Assessment."

Requirements:

In this section, the additional resources necessary to attain the short-term goals are defined.

Tactical Assessment:

The Tactical Assessment is a method of selecting and applying available *resources* toward identified *obstacles* with specific *actions* to achieve resolution.

AUTOMATION PROJECT STRATEGIC AND TACTICAL ASSESSMENT: STRATEGIC ASSESSMENT

1. Misson Statement (Purpose of this project):
   To improve sales enterprise effectiveness and productivity in order to:

2. The Top Five Long-Term Goals (1 – 5 years):
   Identify in two categories: *Effectiveness* and *Productivity*.

3. The Top Five Short-Term Objectives and Expectations (90 days):
   Identify in two categories: *Effectiveness* and *Productivity*.

4. Resources Available:

	Operational	Technical	Advisory
A. Customer			
B. Vendor			
C. Financial			

5. Obstacles Anticipated:

A. Technical

B. Logistics

C. Personnel

D. Financial

6. Additional Requirements:

Sample Strategic and Tactical Assessment

Short-Term Goal Assumptions:

- Ninety-day time frame for achievement/evaluation of objectives
- Primary evaluation criteria are increases in sales effectiveness and productivity
- With products typically requiring more than a thirty-day sell cycle, minimal direct sales increases, if any
- Effectiveness evaluation will generally take precedence over productivity evaluation. For example, it is more important that we are making the "right" or "high-potential" sales calls rather than just more sales calls.

Effectiveness Objectives:

Evaluator: Sales representatives

1. Demonstrate improved customer responsiveness and satisfaction level.

Criteria:

A. Timeliness of response, avoidance of missed calls/errors

2. Improve sales representative organization and territory management effectiveness.

B. Account information accessibility

C. Territory/personal organization enhancements

D. Forward sales cycle movement of qualified prospects and forecasting accuracy

E. Identification/disconnect with low-probability prospects

Evaluator: Sales managers

3. Improve manager's personal effectiveness.

    A. Availability/accessibility/analysis of customer and sales progress data

    B. Personal time usage and management improvements

        1. Personal organization

        2. Reduced reporting load (upward and downward)

        3. Forecast accuracy

4. Improve unit sales effectiveness.

    C. Forward movement of sales opportunities/focus on "right" sales strategies

    D. Improvements in manager to sales rep communications (coaching/planning)

    E. Identification of and early intervention in sales progress obstacles

Evaluator: All

5. Improve process usage, coaching, sales call effectiveness.

PRODUCTIVITY OBJECTIVES:

1. **Increased sales leads "processed"** (for example, qualified/call scheduled or unqualified/deleted)
2. **Increased number of opportunities/accounts evaluated weekly by manager/rep team**
3. **Increase in targeted sales rep-driven marketing programs**
4. **Reduction in time spent by reps and managers in reporting or evaluating available data**
5. **Increase in customer face-to-face time** (managers and sales representatives)

4. SALES NEEDS QUESTIONNAIRE

This questionnaire is a tool to develop an understanding by *non-sales project team members* of the perceptions of sales managers and executives regarding the current and short-term future (one to three years) success factors affecting the sales organization — that is, what does it take to be successful today, what will it take tomorrow, what is standing in the way of achieving the desired level of success? From this we can identify the sales capabilities that would be considered high-value or "big payoff" items in an SFA system. The questionnaire focuses on six main areas of the sales operation: the organization, the marketplace, sales management, and sales representatives.

This is a "sales" questionnaire, not a "sales automation" questionnaire. Its approach is to discuss the sales environment with key senior sales executives — what customers are going to be looking for (other than pure product) and how the company will attempt to provide it through sales operations.

This questionnaire is designed to be a discussion guide, not a "fill-in-the-blanks" assessment. Its questions are meant as a guide for the interviewer to help identify key points that need to be considered in developing any sales improvement process or system.

AGENDA

In this questionnaire the focus is on the following topic areas:

Organization — The company profile and structure

Customer — Profiles of why customers buy or quit buying.

Marketplace — How have customer expectations, your sales approach, and competitive pressures changed? Why? How will they change in the future? What is your future strategy for success?

Sales Representatives — Profiles of successful and unsuccessful salespeople. What are the critical skills and capabilities they will need to meet future challenges?

Sales Managers — Profiles of successful and unsuccessful sales managers. What are the critical skills and capabilities they will need to meet future challenges?

The Crystal Ball — What will stand in the way of the sales organization in achieving its future goals, and what is your strategy to address it?

COMPANY PROFILE

Company: _____

Industry: _____

Products/Services: _____

Selling Style:

( ) large account

( ) small/medium

( ) distributor/reseller

( ) indirect or contract

( ) retail

Number of Salespeople: _____ Average Years Experience: _____

Number of Managers: _____

What is your sales philosophy?

What is your source of competitive edge? (Value/Feature)

How has this changed in the last five years?

How will this change in the next five years?

CUSTOMER PROFILE

Describe a typical customer of your company. Will this change in the future? How?

What are the primary sources of business? (Direct mail, cold calls, repeat customers, etc.)
Do you expect these to continue to be the primary sources in the future? What are you doing to maximize their effectiveness?

Why do they buy from you rather than your competitor?

Why do they quit buying?

How do you assure long-term customer satisfaction?

What would your customers say you do very well?

What would your customers say you could do better?

How are you addressing this today? How will you address it in the future?

What are your current and future strategies to keep and grow your current customers?

THE MARKETPLACE

What is your current market position? (leader, contender, market share increasing/decreasing)

What factors have done the most to make you successful, that is, win business?

What factors have caused or contributed to sales losses?

How are you addressing these today?

How will these win/loss factors change from competition, economics, and customer expectations?

What will be your long-term strategy to address these?

THE SALES ORGANIZATION

How is success measured: revenue attainment, profitability, customer satisfaction?
Is this changing and how?

How are salespeople and managers compensated? Will this change and how?

As an organization, what are the greatest strengths that contribute to meeting sales goals?

How do salespeople spend their time weekly (as a percentage)?

_____ direct selling (face-to-face)

_____ customer service or support

_____ telephone

_____ travel

_____ administration (reports, forms, etc.)

_____ sales meetings, coaching sessions

What are the greatest inefficiencies in sales and marketing, and what is the impact of these inefficiencies?

What do salespeople need that they do not currently have to maximize their productivity and efficiency?

In addition to the salesperson, who in your company also "touches" the customer?

Is team selling a current or future requirement? How would you rate the effectiveness of current programs and why?

THE SALES REPRESENTATIVES

How would you define your selling process or model? Do you anticipate that this will change? What are its strengths and weaknesses?

What are the chief characteristics of your successful salespeople today? Has this changed from the past? How will it change in the future? How will you help them adapt?

Why do salespeople fail?

Aside from personal skills or product issues, what obstacles stand in the way of your salespeople? (organizational, demographics, financial, informational, or other)

As you hire new sales reps in the future, what skills or experience will you look for, and how has this changed?

What skills are the most critical to develop in a trainee? How do you do this?

Do you actively use a sales planning methodology? What is its value to you? What percentage of the salespeople consistently utilize it?

Do you actively use a sales automation system? What is its value to you? What percentage of the salespeople consistently utilize it?

THE SALES MANAGERS

What are the chief characteristics of your successful sales managers today? Has this changed from the past? How will it change in the future? How will you help them adapt?

Why do sales managers fail?

Aside from personal skills or product issues, what obstacles stand in the way of your sales managers? (organizational, demographics, financial, informational, or other)

As you promote new managers in the future, what skills or experience will you look for, and how has this changed?

What skills are the most critical to develop in a manager? How do you do this?

Do you actively use a sales planning methodology? What is its value to you? What percentage of the sales mangers consistently utilize it?

Do you actively use a sales automation system? What is its value to you? What percentage of the sales managers consistently utilize it and how?

SALES FORCE AUTOMATION

What is your opinion of the ability of SFA to improve the following?

- Sales rep productivity/effectiveness

- Sales management productivity/effectiveness

- Benefit to corporate management

- Marketing focus

- Customer satisfaction

What should the sales automation system of the future do?

5. STRATEGY MAPPING FORMS

TERRITORY AND MARKET PLANNER

Territory/Market Assessment:

A. Long-Term Goals (1 – 3 years)

1. General Revenue Goals

Current Year 1	Year 2	Year 3

2. Product-Line Revenue Goals

Product	Current Year 1	Year 2	Year 3

3. Known Key Accounts/Prospects in Territory/Market

Account	Customer Y/N	Products	$ Potential	Competitor
1.				
2.				
3.				
4.				
5.				
6.				
7.				
8.				
9.				
10.				

4. Competition

Competitor	Strength	Weakness
1.		
2.		
3.		
4.		
5.		

5. Personal Long-Term Goals

1.

2.

3.

4.

5.

B. Short-Term Goals (Current year)

1. Revenue Goals

1st Quarter	2nd Quarter	3rd Quarter	4th Quarter
$	$	$	$

2. Product-Line Revenue Goals

Product	Units	Revenue $	

3. Current Year Focus Accounts

Account	Opportunity	Revenue $	Active Y/N
1.			
2.			
3.			
4.			
5.			

4. Personal Short-Term Goals

1.

2.

3.

4.

5.

C. Resource/Obstacle Assessment

Resources Available to Make Short-Term Goals

Resources/Obstacles	Resource	Obstacle
Demographics (sufficient accounts/opportunities identified)		
Territory Accessibility (ease of coverage)		
Personal Selling Skills (strong or weak)		
Product Knowledge (strong or weak)		
Business Development Skills (strong or weak)		
Pre-Sales Support: technical (strong or weak)		
Pre-Sales Support: management (strong or weak)		
Pre-Sales Support: marketing (strong or weak)		
Post-Sale Support/Implementation		
Account Knowledge (industry, business goals, defined needs)		
Account/Key Contact Access (decision makers)		
Competitive Customer Base (satisfied or vulnerable)		
Competitive Marketing Presence (active or inactive)		
Financial Resources (expense budget, etc.)		

D. Tactics/Requirements
(Strategies to develop strengths and resolve obstacles)

Demographics (sufficient accounts/opportunities):

Territory Accessibility (ease of coverage):

Personal Selling Skills:

Product Knowledge:

Business Development Skills:

Pre-Sales Support: Technical:

Pre-Sales Support: Management:

Pre-Sales Support: Marketing:

Post-Sale Support/Implementation:

Account Knowledge (industry, business goals, defined needs):

Account/Key Contact Access (decision makers):

Competitive Customer Base:

Competitive Marketing Presence:

Financial Resources:

E. Marketplace Perceived-Value Analysis (Nine business needs)

Value ("We provide our customers ... .")	Provided?	Perception
Product or service for resale		
Funding (sales, investment, terms, etc.)		
Operations (physical operation of the business)		
Competitive Advantage — increase		
Customer Satisfaction — increase		
Information — uniquely available		
Expertise — not available internally		
Profits — increase		
Opportunity — increase sales opportunities		
	TOP 3 TOTAL	

F. Territory Advantage/Vulnerability Position

Score	Position
11–15	High Competitive Advantage/Low Vulnerability to Competitive Intrusion
6–10	Competitive Parity, No Perceived Advantage, Moderate Vulnerability
0–5	Competitive Disadvantage/High Vulnerability to Competitive Intrusion

G. Top Three "One-Point Plan"

Detail strategy to improve "Top 3" selected value perceptions by 1 point:

MAJOR ACCOUNT PLAN

PART 1: KEY ACCOUNT PROFILE
KEY ACCOUNT: _____

A. Industry

A. Industry	Market Served	$ Revenue	Position	Products

Market Position: G = Growing, S = Stable, D = Declining

B. Corporate Organization

Company	P/S/A/D	Location	Products	Position	Customer Y/N

P/S/A/D: P = Parent, S = Subsidiary, A = Affiliate, D = Division
Market Position: G = Growing, S = Stable, D = Declining

C. Key Contact Analysis

Contact	Title	Access Y/N	S/O/A	Role in Decisions
1.				
2.				
3.				
4.				
5.				
6.				
7.				
8.				

S/O/A: S = Support, O = Open, A = Against

D. Previous Sales Summary

Date	Product	Dept/Div.	$ Revenue	Result

PART 2: ACCOUNT DEVELOPMENT PLANNER
KEY ACCOUNT: _____

A. Long-Term Goals (1–3 years)

1. General Revenue Goals

Current Year 1	Year 2	Year 3

2. Product-Line Revenue Goals

Product	Current Year 1	Year 2	Year 3

3. Potential Long-Term Sales Opportunities in This Account

Opportunity	Active Y/N	Products	$ Potential	Competitor
1.				
2.				
3.				
4.				
5.				
6.				
7.				
8.				
9.				
10.				

4. Competition in This Account

Competitor	Strength	Weakness
1.		
2.		
3.		
4.		
5.		

5. Other Long-Term Account Development Goals

1.

2.

3.

4.

5.

B. Short-Term Account Goals (current year)

1. Revenue Goals

1st Quarter	2nd Quarter	3rd Quarter	4th Quarter

2. Product-Line Revenue Goals

Product	Units	Revenue $

3. Current Year Focus Sales Opportunities

Opportunity	Description	Revenue $	Active Y/N
1.			
2.			
3.			
4.			
5.			

4. Other Short-Term Account Development Goals

1.

2.

3.

4.

5.

C. Resource/Obstacle Assessment

Resources Available to Make Short-Term Goals

Resources/Obstacles	Resource	Obstacle
Potential (sufficient opportunities for sales investment)		
Account Accessibility (ease of coverage)		
Personal Selling Skills		
Product Knowledge (related to account industry/application)		
Account Development Skills		
Pre-Sales Support: technical		
Pre-Sales Support: management		
Pre-Sales Support: marketing		
Post-Sale Support/Implementation		
Account Knowledge (industry, business goals, defined needs)		
Account/Key Contact Access (decision makers)		
Competitive Install/customer Satisfaction		
Competitive Marketing Presence		
Financial Resources (expense budget, etc.)		

D. Tactics/Requirements
(Strategies to develop strengths and resolve obstacles)

Potential (sufficient opportunities):

Account Accessibility (ease of coverage):

Personal Selling Skills:

Product Knowledge (customer industry/needs/application):

Account Development Skills:

Pre-Sales Support: Technical:

Pre-Sales Support: Management:

Pre-Sales Support: Marketing:

Post-Sale Support/Implementation:

Account Knowledge (industry, business goals, defined needs and process):

Account/Key Contact Access (decision makers):

Competitive Install and Customer Satisfaction:

Competitive Marketing Presence:

Financial Resources:

E. Account Perceived-Value Analysis (Nine business needs)

Value ("We provide this account … .")	Provided?	Perception
Product or service for resale		
Funding (sales, investment, terms, etc.)		
Operations (physical operation of the business)		
Competitive Advantage — increase		
Customer Satisfaction — increase		
Information — uniquely available		
Expertise — not available internally		
Profits — increase		
Opportunity — increase sales opportunities		
	TOP 3 TOTAL	

F. Account Advantage/Vulnerability Position

Score	Position
11 – 15	High Competitive Advantage/Low Vulnerability to Competitive Intrusion
6 – 10	Competitive Parity, No Perceived Advantage, Moderate Vulnerability
0 – 5	Competitive Disadvantage/High Vulnerability to Competitive Intrusion

G. Key Competitor Perceived-Value Analysis (Nine business needs)

Value ("They provide this account....")	Provided?	Perception
Product or Service for Resale		
Funding (sales, investment, terms, etc.)		
Operations (physical operation of the business)		
Competitive Advantage — increase		
Customer Satisfaction — increase		
Information — uniquely available		
Expertise — not available internally		
Profits — increase		
Opportunity — increase sales opportunities		
	TOP 3 TOTAL	

H. Competitor Vulnerability Targets

Value	Strategy

I. Top Three "One-Point Plan"

Detail strategy to improve "Top 3" selected value perceptions by 1 point:

STRATEGY MAP OPPORTUNITY PLAN

KEY ACCOUNT: _____

OPPORTUNITY TITLE: _____

Opportunity	**Assessment**
Prospect event or situation that created this opportunity	
Customer-perceived need	
Customer vision of optimal solution and anticipated results	(Attach technical requirements summary.)
Funding source budgeted? Available?	
Decision process and date	

"Driver" contact and

personal motive

Proposed product solution

Revenue $$

Alignment with prospect

needs and buy motive

OPPORTUNITY CONTACT ANALYSIS

Contact	Title	Access	Support	Buyer Role
1.				
2.				
3.				
4.				
5.				
6.				
7.				
8.				

Support: S = Support, O = Open, A = Against

Role: Decision maker, Influencer, Approver, Observer, Advocate, Power advocate

** Do we have access to decision-making power? _____

Key Opportunity Planning

Strategic Value of this Opportunity

Potential Follow-on Sales Opportunity Leveraged by this Opportunity

Opportunity	Active Y/N	Products	$ Potential	Competitor
1.				
2.				
3.				
4.				
5.				
6.				
7.				
8.				
9.				
10.				

Opportunity Perceived-Value Analysis (Nine business needs)

Value ("We provide this account ... .")	Provided?	Perception
Product or service for resale		
Funding (sales, investment, terms, etc.)		
Operations (physical operation of the business)		
Competitive Advantage — increase		
Customer Satisfaction — increase		
Information — uniquely available		
Expertise — not available internally		
Profits — increase		
Opportunity — increase sales opportunities		
	TOP 3 TOTAL	

Opportunity Advantage/Vulnerability Position

Score	Position
11–15	High Competitive Advantage/Low Vulnerability to Competitive Intrusion
6–10	Competitive Parity, No Perceived Advantage, Moderate Vulnerability
0–5	Competitive Disadvantage/High Vulnerability to Competitive Intrusion

Key Competitor Perceived-Value Analysis (Nine business needs)

Value ("They provide this account ... .")	Provided?	Perception
Product or service for resale		
Funding (sales, investment, terms, etc.)		
Operations (physical operation of the business)		
Competitive Advantage — increase		
Customer Satisfaction — increase		
Information — uniquely available		
Expertise — not available internally		
Profits — increase		
Opportunity — increase sales opportunities		
	TOP 3 TOTAL	

Competitor Vulnerability Targets

Value	Strategy	

Top Three "One-Point Plan"

Detail strategy to improve "Top 3" selected value perceptions by 1 point:

STRATEGY MAP
BEST/NEXT SEQUENCE OF SALES TACTICS

SEQUENCE:

CONTACT:

TITLE:

BUYER ROLE:

    1. RECOGNITION

    2. VISION

    3. RE-VISION

    4. RE-SOLUTION

BEST/NEXT TACTIC

SEQUENCE:

CONTACT:

TITLE:

BUYER ROLE:

    1. RECOGNITION

    2. VISION

    3. RE-VISION

    4. RE-SOLUTION

BEST/NEXT TACTIC

SEQUENCE: _____

CONTACT: _____

TITLE: _____

BUYER ROLE: _____

    1. RECOGNITION

_____

    2. VISION

_____

    3. RE-VISION

_____

    4. RE-SOLUTION

_____

BEST/NEXT TACTIC

CHAPTER 9

A SALES AUTOMATION SAMPLER

I am frequently asked, "What sales automation package do you recommend?" I have my favorite systems that I believe are rich in capabilities, developed by companies that do an excellent job of supporting their customers. The problem is, however, that the answer just isn't that easy. It really depends on what you need. And with almost 1,000 vendors in the marketplace, there are at least ten viable choices for whatever you need.

When we started planning this book, the publisher asked me to select a single sales automation system that I thought represented what a system should be and that most closely demonstrated the capability to support the concepts we have discussed throughout *The Sales Manager/Sales Automation Equation*.

It is an impossible task to make that kind of choice because there are many excellent SFA providers on the market, any of whom may fit the specific needs of a wide variety of customers. Brock International, headquartered in Atlanta, is one of the oldest vendors in this still young industry and has created an enviable record of success with its customers, particularly in the telesales environment. Another is Aurum, a company that is coming on fast in the marketplace and that I consider an industry leader — very strong in the large corporate areas. And there are many, many others. I apologize in advance to all the fine vendors whose products there wasn't space to mention.

In the end I asked Howard Getson, CEO of IntellAgent Control Corporation of Dallas, Texas, to share his views and philosophy of sales automation and to profile their product, IntellAgent Control®. Howard and his company share much of my vision of what a sales automation system should be and how it should be used. Their newest product release directly supports STRATEGY MAPPING.

A BIT OF BACKGROUND

In 1995 I met Howard Getson, at an expert panel sponsored by IBM, on which we were both sitting. Earlier I had met Doug Fenn and Mike Goode, also of the same company, at a series of automation seminars sponsored by Apple Computer. We shared a similar vision of sales automation and a belief that the next generation of sales automation would come through the effective marriage of powerful new technologies with powerful new selling methodologies.

Doug had said to me, "We ought to sit down some time and figure out how we can work together. Let me know the next time you're coming through Dallas." A few months later, we finally did meet and developed a pilot strategy for integrating STRATEGY MAPPING as a free-standing module within the product, IntellAgent Control. At this writing, that task continues with great mutual enthusiasm.

A few product notes. IntellAgent Control is a comprehensive sales automation system that has been installed in both large and small sales organizations. The product has account, opportunity, and contact management capabilities and corporate-wide data communications ability. It is based on the Lotus Notes technology.

INTELLAGENT CONTROL

BY
HOWARD M. GETSON
PRESIDENT AND CEO
INTELLAGENT CONTROL CORPORATION

INTRODUCTION

We designed IntellAgent Control to be as simple to use as a piece of paper and a pencil. The deliberately simple design encourages exploration. One of the key design objectives was to have the system flow naturally and seem to anticipate the user's next move. We wanted to make the system work the way users (salespeople, managers, and sales executives) think, so we told the developers to make forms always fit on one screen so that a user would never have to scroll up or down or wonder where to look for information.

What we've created is a clean look and feel, with strong visual cues that guide salespeople to take the right steps. For example, at the top of every screen is a graphic element that explains where you are, such as a Company Profile, an Opportunity Plan, or a Contact Profile. In the upper right-hand corner of each screen, we have buttons that help you do things like print, exit, save, or cancel. We're very proud of a rule-based artificial intelligence system that understands who you are and what you're trying to do. These intelligent buttons are located at the bottom of the screen and highlight the next six (or fewer) appropriate steps. It is easy to take action no matter where you are in the system.

Basic customer information and critical activities are translated into the following categories.

THE COMPANY PROFILE

The Company Profile contains the information typically found on a business card. It displays the address, city, state, zip, and phone numbers for the company. Of course, there is room for other information relevant to the company, such as an account number, a distin-

---

(The following "mini-demo" and product data were provided courtesy of IntellAgent Control Corporation. The writer and the publisher of this book make no representations of the accuracy of the information contained within this material nor do they guarantee the appropriateness of the products and services described for any specific purchaser.)

---

guishing "status" indicator (such as "client," "prospect," etc.). In addition to the status of an account, you may also want to show what region the account is in, who is responsible for it, or even who the primary contacts are in that company.

FIGURE 9.1. THE COMPANY PROFILE

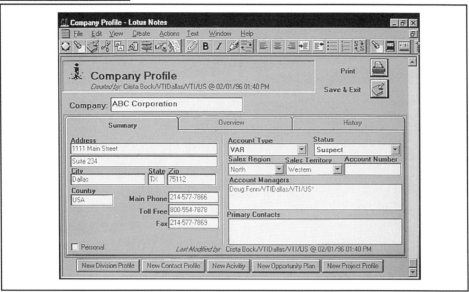

Notice how we use "tabs" to help users focus on certain information. Tabs are another component of a pleasant, uncluttered user environment. With tabs it is easy for users to switch to different one-page forms without forcing them to use menus or complex keyboard commands. So on a Company Profile, clicking on the Overview tab selectively reveals only the pertinent fields, based on the company's account type, status, or other differentiator chosen by the user.

The system's intelligence is based on the "rules" you set. Part of the design philosophy is to build screens based on logical "chunks" of information. We try to choose collections of data that naturally occur together. Another filtering technique is to attempt to limit the display of anything other than what the user expects to see. For example, people in sales want to view different data than people in the accounting department. This principle also applies when users fill out forms. We try very hard to ask only those questions the users would know the answers to when they are initially asked to fill out the form. Why? Because we have learned that asking questions to which users have no immediate answers can actually discourage use. In short, the design of IntellAgent Control attempts to make sure that users always have a chance to successfully complete each task and then are prompted to take further action. We believe that technology accounts for only 20% of the "success equation" for sales automation and that 80% is cultural sociology. In other words, the system needs to work the way people think!

Now it is time to investigate the intelligent buttons located at the bottom of the screen and their related actions. From the Company Profile, these buttons prompt users to create division and contact profiles or to create activities. In many "contact management systems" users can become confused about whether something is a "call," a "meeting," a "to-do," a "note," a "history item," or an "activity." In our system there is really only one step, and it is called an Activity. With one click of an intelligent button, you are in a notepad and are ready to record information. IntellAgent Control brings up information about date, time, and the event. If the "activity" requires scheduling an event for someone other than yourself, the system will automatically create an electronic mail message alerting that person and providing him or her a hypertext link to this account's database file—even if he or she is not normally connected to this system. Activities can also be viewed in a graphic calendar format, as well as in Views, or sorted by responsible person, due date, company, manager, or any other relevant reporting criteria. In short, data become intelligence.

VIEWS

Users access information within the database from various perspectives, called "Views." One way to look at Views is as a collection of forms. The forms are actually electronic representations of documents, whether they are a business card, a call report, a contact profile, or an opportunity. The base system contains many predefined Views, yet it is open to addition or modification. Views let users select, sort, and categorize the information they need. Views may also show subtotals, average, and percentage statistics. While most are "public" (accessible to any authorized user), users may also create private Views that are not stored in the public database. Database designers may also restrict access to particular documents by assigning users and documents specific database privileges.

FIGURE 9.2. VIEWS

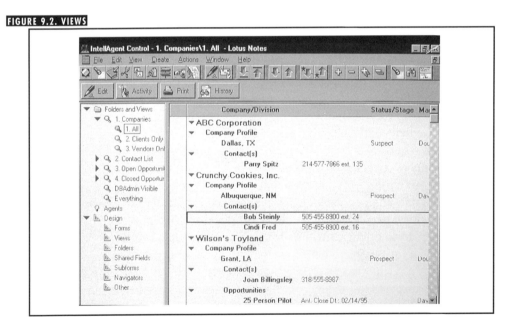

Examples of Views might be a list of companies or only a rep's clients or prospects. Another View could list contacts by first name, last name, or by the company for which they work. You might also want to look at a list of open opportunities (your sales funnel or "pipeline") by anticipated close date, revenue, probability, region, salesperson, product, or any other criterion. Views can even be created related to events that have already happened — deals closed in a quarter, lead performance, win/loss ratios, or competitors. These "performance-tracking views" allow you to track the characteristics of deals that you have won or lost in ways that are most meaningful — to understand how we won or why we lost (and avoid having it happen again).

THE OPPORTUNITY FORM: TEAM SELLING IN ACTION

Instead of looking at a company or a contact, let's open an opportunity. Notice that the Opportunity Plan looks very much like a Company Profile. There is a graphic element at the top that says "Opportunity Plan." The form clearly shows when it was created, who created it, and when it was last modified. True to form, there are administrative buttons in the upper right-hand corner that let you do things, such as print, exit, save, or cancel. And shown at the bottom are the intelligent buttons. Based on the type of opportunity and the stage the deal is in, the buttons lead users to the most appropriate next steps.

FIGURE 9.3. THE OPPORTUNITY PLAN

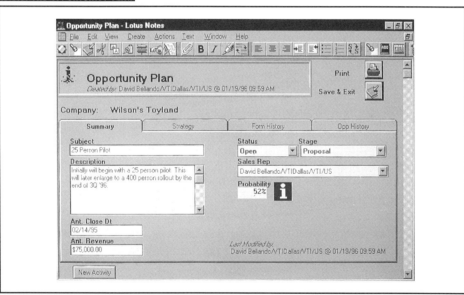

On the initial Opportunity Plan screen, the only information requested about the forecast is "probability," "anticipated close date," and "amount." Why? Because that information is probably all a salesperson will know when he or she first creates the opportunity. Intelligent buttons branch to "strategy" and other information when you are ready!

IntellAgent Control has an interactive probability calculator for deals. When you choose this option, the system presents you with a series of questions that you design for your specific selling environment. In our case, since we sell Lotus Notes and IntellAgent Control, we ask questions such as, "Does the prospect have Notes installed?" We also help our people focus on the competition, the buying influences, and the progress of the deal. For example, in the progress section we ask questions that include "Have we completed a demonstration?" "Have they requested a proposal?" "Have we entered negotiations?" By answering these questions, we create a weighted average probability that is much like a credit score. Ultimately, it tells you that you have a certain percentage chance of winning the deal.

The system also uses rule-based intelligence to pick appropriate work flows or sales processes based on the product or service chosen. The process is made up of various rules that can have time frames and activities related to them. For example, if you have completed the "qualification" stage and the next step is proposal, the system could automatically recalculate the anticipated closing date, assign critical activities, and mail appropriate messages to people alerting them to current status and required actions.

Likewise, the system can automatically assign relevant tasks or allow different people to read, edit, or otherwise access this file based on probability. The result is that the opportunity moves to the right person at the right time. If you have a telemarketing group, an inside sales group, and an outside sales group, you can automatically move opportunities through the funnel to each one at the right time.

There are also tabs at the top of the Opportunity Plan. One is for the Summary, which includes the base description, the forecast, and the sales process. Another tab is for Strategy. The Strategy tab is interesting because it brings up a relevant form based on the status and stage of the deal. This capability is included with the standard product, yet it can be added to or modified to support your unique processes and/or methodologies.

Out of the box, IntellAgent Control ships with generic strategy documents to help people identify decision makers, their buying triggers, and the best next steps to pursue. However, a real advantage of using a flexible, open system, such as IntellAgent Control, is that you can now add "methodology templates" that suit the way your company sells. For example, IntellAgent Control now directly supports Labyrinth Research's STRATEGY MAPPING. So, in addition to a simple shared work group account, task, and opportunity management system, companies can get the benefit of world-class strategy and BEST/NEXT planning to enable even novice users to perform like experts.

FIGURE 9.4. THE CONTACT PROFILE

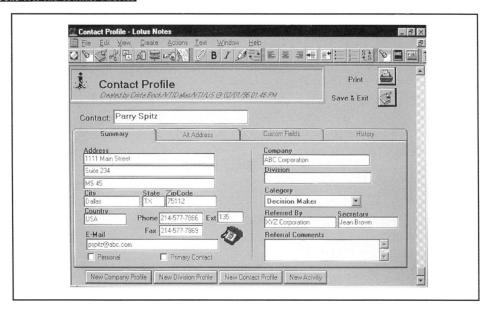

THE CONTACT PROFILE

The next step is to link the opportunity back to people. As you link various customer or prospect personnel into their decision-making roles in the buying process, we give you a one-click access to their contact profile. Again, the contact profile fits on a single screen and has all the normal buttons, as well as the look and feel of the rest of the system. Here, however, you can write a letter, send a fax, dial the telephone, or look at the history for the individual selected. Throughout the system, the intelligent buttons allow you access in one click to all the history about a company or everything anyone has done, said, or promised about an opportunity. The company-to-company commitments are an accumulation of anything anyone has done, said, or promised to another individual. In this way, whether you're looking at the global strategy or the specific tactics for an individual call plan, you'll get exactly what you want, the way you need it.

OTHER MODULES IN THE INTELLAGENT CONTROL SYSTEM

IntellAgent Control acts as the hub of the IntellAgent Control system. It is where you store information about the accounts you deal with, the opportunities you have with those accounts, the projects or the commitments you make, and the ways you meet those commitments. We offer other databases in the system to deal with other targeted business solutions related to sales, marketing, and customer service.

Sales force automation is a lot more than mere contact management. Contact managers are on target for helping people manage contacts, activity, and time. However, in an organization, you're looking more at the synergies of group communication, collaboration, and coordination. This involves executive information systems with forecasting and ratio analysis, project management systems that track commitments and how they are met, expense tracking and other applications that reduce "administrivia." Other relevant modules might include a sales handbook, group scheduling databases, marketing encyclopedias, and data warehouses.

One of the database templates offered in the IntellAgent Control system is IntellAgent Document Control. This is a repository for proposals, presentations, price lists, or other marketing and communication documents. Not only does this system conform to the same look and feel as the rest of the system, but also it has a built-in document work flow so that as a piece of work goes from "draft" to "work group review" to "complete" to "obsolete," the system automatically changes who can edit and who can read the document. When you are ready, it can even send your document to your Internet site for public availability.

The reason IntellAgent Control offers other modules besides the basic account database is that individual users need a "what's in it for me?" win for each of them. If they look at the system as "Big Brother is watching" and only as a measurement tool, there's no incentive for them to become proficient. On the other hand, by giving them targeted business tools to help them perform better, by giving them access to the most accurate and timely product information on pricing, product availability, your business partners, or a new product information piece, you empower them to sell more and put more money in their own pockets.

ROLL-OUT STRATEGIES

Another reason IntellAgent Control uses a modular approach is that companies can choose to roll out the system using the basic IntellAgent Control database and various combinations of the modules over time. People start with one or two simple databases and, as they move up the technology adoption curve, they add additional tools. A key point here is that the technology is not important—what is important is how it helps people perform better.

One key suggestion is, rather than roll out the modules by themselves, make sure that people in an organization fill the modules with content that is appropriate for an individual. Take, for example, IntellAgent Document Control. The database itself is irrelevant to the end-user, unless it contains information that will help him or her sell better. So before you roll it out, make sure you include "selling information," such as biographies of key executives, reprints of various articles, white papers that explain why your service or product is better than a competitor's, and other similar information. This is what salespeople want and need, not just the repository itself.

The same rationale goes for Competitive IntellAgents. The concept of the database is interesting, but it must contain relevant data that are updated on a regular basis. Make sure someone in your organization is responsible for putting information in, and also make sure you encourage other people throughout the organization to input information. The result is that this becomes a dynamic, living, breathing system. You want people at the highest and lowest levels of your company to feel that they have ownership of that information and that, as they find information relevant to other people, they are encouraged and enabled to share it easily. Competitive IntellAgents enables them to enter it once and share it with everyone.

Finally, with IntellAgent Control, make sure that before you roll it out to end users, it has their accounts, their opportunities, and their historical data, so that they understand how the system works in the context of their world. The database in and of itself is interesting only to technical enthusiasts. To ensure success, you have to make it interesting to the end users. The only things interesting to end users are their accounts and the ability to put more money in their pockets using the benefits of a selling tool such as IntellAgent Control.

ABOUT INTELLAGENT CONTROL CORPORATION

IntellAgent Control Corporation, a leader in developing groupware solutions for sales, marketing, and service sectors, is a Lotus Premium Business Partner. The core product, the IntellAgent Control System™, is a Lotus Notes®-based, enterprise-wide work-group solution for account, project, and opportunity management. IntellAgent Control is a full-featured software company with customer service, quality assurance, technical support, and a nation-wide network of business partners. The company was founded in 1991 as Veritas Technologies, Inc., and it commercially introduced IntellAgent Control in 1993. The company released version 4 of IntellAgent Control in 1996.

IntellAgent Control is used for sales force automation by many Fortune 1000 firms in various industries. The IntellAgent Control System includes the central database, IntellAgent Control, plus associated modules for distribution of product and sales information, document management, selective replication with personal information managers (such as ACT!® and Goldmine®), software storage, distribution of competitive information, and secure database administration. All modules are shipped with the core program at no extra cost to clients with maintenance agreements.

IntellAgent Control and all related marks are the property of IntellAgent Control Corporation. All other marks are the property of their respective companies.

INDEX

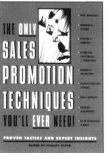

YES! Send me the book(s) I have checked. I understand that if I am not completely satisfied, I may return the book(s) within 30 days for a full refund. (Shipping and handling charges will be added to your invoice. IL residents please add 8.75% tax; IN residents add 5% tax; Canadian residents add 7.5% GST.)

☐ *185 Sales Tips for Sure-Fire Success*
  $21.50; Book code 1233

☐ *The Idea-a-Day Guide to Super Selling and Customer Service*
  $21.50; Book code 1185

☐ *The Only Sales Promotion Techniques You'll Ever Need!*
  $39.95; Book code 1255

☐ *The Greatest Direct Mail Sales Letters of All Time*
  $69.95; Book code 1239

☐ *Questions That Make the Sale*
  $21.95; Book code 1196

Bill my: ☐ VISA ☐ MasterCard ☐ American Express ☐ Optima ☐ Company

Card Number _____ Exp. Date _____

Name _____

Title _____

Company _____

Address _____

City/State/Zip _____

Signature _____

Phone (   ) _____

Fax Number (   ) _____

E-mail _____

(Signature and phone number necessary to process order.)   96-5505

Copies may be ordered from your bookseller or from Dartnell.
Prices subject to change without notice.
To order from Dartnell, call toll free (800) 621-5463,
or fax us your order (800) 327-8635.

DARTNELL
4660 N RAVENSWOOD AVE, CHICAGO, IL 60640-4595